INDEX

PAGE 1:	Introduction.
PAGE 2:	Indian Food Terms.
PAGE 5:	Language Guide
PAGE 10:	Conversions.
PAGE 11:	The Basics
PAGE 12:	Chutneys.
PAGE 18:	The Basics
PAGE 26:	Raitas
PAGE 29:	Breads.
PAGE 35:	Appetisers.
PAGE 41:	Soups.
PAGE 45:	Salads.
PAGE 49:	Kebabs.
PAGE 52:	Snacks.
PAGE 57:	Meat Dishes.
PAGE 71:	Fish Dishes.
PAGE 73:	Vegetarian
PAGE 110:	Deserts.
PAGE 123:	Drinks

Indian food terms

Given below are some food items with a native touch, but common to India. Also find some item names that are called differently.

Item	Description
Alu	Potato
Atta	Flour
Badusha	A sweet made of refined flour, fried in ghee and dipped in sugar syrup
Bathura	A moon shaped fried snack made of wheat flour and fried in oil to puff. Normally taken with a side dish namely 'Chole'
Batter	Mixture of flour and water, stirred or beaten to form a thin/thick paste.
Bhajia	A snack made of sliced vegetable dipped in bengal gram flour and deep fried to crispy form
Bhaji	Another term for green vegetables
Bhelpuri	A snack made of puffed rice, chopped onion, mild spices and pulses
Bhujia	A dish prepared in minced form
Bhurta	A dish made of vegetable, baked on heat or fire and subsequently mashed to prepare the dish
Bonda	A round shaped deep-fried snack that consists of potato curry covered with a layer of bengal gram batter
Boondi	Sieved batter of bengal gram flour fried to crispy form in the shape of pearls
Biryani	A specific method of rice preparation with select vegetables and aromatic spices
Burfi	A sweet made in the form of a thin soft cake
Biryani pathha	Bay leaf
Chapati	A thin layer of pressed wheat flour dough, baked on a flat pan with very little oil. The same baked without oil is termed as 'phulka'
Chenna	Curdled cow milk in solidified form used as a main ingredient for preparation of some sweets also known as bengali sweets
Chutney	A hot/spicy dish made of fried and ground spices with a choice of vegetables / greens
Chole	An exclusive spicy side dish that is taken with puri or bathura
Chumchum	A syrup filled spongy milk sweet
Chuka	Country sorrel
Chick peas	Whole bengal gram
Curry powder	Dry ground powder made of select aromatic spices and pulses used in curries
Curd	Yoghurt
Dal	A dish made of cooked pulses with different vegetables in variant flavors
Dosa	A moon shaped snack made of fermented batter, baked with little oil in the form of a thin pan cake
Dhum	The process of cooking a dish with the vessel covered and heat from both ends
Dhokla	Steam cooked semolina puffs with mild spices
Deep fry	A method of frying vegetable or a snack
Garam masala	Dry powder made of aromatic spices used in little quantity in curries or rice
Eatable camphor	A diluted form of eatable camphor used in preparation of sweets
Egg plant	Brinjal
Gulab jamun	A soft round shaped sweet made of milk powder or solidified milk, deep fried in ghee and soaked in sugar syrup
Ghee	Clarified butter
Griddle	A flat metal plate similar to skillet
Gravy	A dish with a large quantity of thick paste made of ground spices or vegetables
Grating	Shredding vegetables with the help of a vegetable grater
Garnish	Decoration given to a food item
Halwa	A sweet in the form of thick jelly, made of ghee and flour in different flavors
Idli	A snack made of fermented batter poured in small quantities into a sieved plate(

	idly stand) and then steam cooked
Ivy gourd	Gerkin
Jaggery	Processed sugar cane juice in solidified form
Jilebi	A sweet made of refined flour batter, fermented and then deep fried in ghee and dipped in sugar syrup
Jhangri	A sweet made of black gram batter, deep fried in ghee and soaked in sugar syrup
Kaja flat	A sweet made of refined flour dough formed into layers, deep fried in ghee and soaked in sugar syrup
Kaja round	A tube shaped sweet made of refined flour dough deep fried in ghee and filled with sugar syrup
Kesari	A soft light sweet made of semolina or vermicelli
Khara	Another term for hot or spicy snacks
Kheer	A sweet made of nuts and condiments in different flavors. Similar to a pudding.
Khoa	Sugarless solidified milk
Koottu	A mild dal variety with a choice of vegetables
Kurma	A spicy curry made of thick gravy and a variety of vegetables
Khofta	Minced vegetables and flour mixture fried in oil as small pieces for final preparation of a curry
Laddu	A traditional round shaped sweet made in different flavors and sizes
Lassi	Sweet buttermilk
Masala	Dry or wet ground powder/paste that consists of various spices / pulses / pungent vegetables. Used as add on flavor to curries or rice.
Namkeen	A snack variety with a combination of pungency, sourness and sweet
Nan	A typical Indian oven to bake pressed wheat flour dough similar to chpati
Okra	Ladies finger
Pannir	Curdled milk in solidified form
Paratha	Rolled wheat or refined flour dough that form into layers and in the shape of a moon or triangle. It is baked on a flat pan with ghee or oil and a choice of vegetables or greens
Papad	Sun dried hard pressed gram flour dough in the form of a moon with a choice of flavors. Can subsequently roasted on heat or deep fried in oil
Payasam	A traditional liquid milk sweet made in different flavors
Pulao	A rice dish cooked with a choice of vegetables and aromatic spices
Peanut	Groundnut
Puri	Moon shaped wheat flour dough, pressed to small sizes and fried in oil with porous formation
Pulusu	A soup variety of thick cooked gram with mild spices and vegetables
Pakora/Pakoda	A snack made with a choice of vegetables, mixed in bengal gram flour and deep fried in oil to small pieces of crispy form
Riata	Softened curd with a choice of vegetables and mild spices mixture
Rasam	A digestive water soup in different flavors with ground pepper and coriander powder
Rasgolla	A round shaped spongy sweet made of curdled milk with lots of sugar syrup
Rawa	Semolina
Sambar	A thick soup variety prepared with cooked red gram and a choice of vegetables
Samosa	A cone shaped popular snack made of potato and peas curry rolled in flour dough and deep fried in oil.
Shrikand	A sweet made with smoothened curd and nutmeg
Semiya	Vermicelli
Sandesh	A milk sweet
Sesame	Gingely seeds
Sev	A snack made of bengal gram flour resembling vermicelli
Syrup	Sugar boiled in water to form a thin liquid of one or two string drops
Subzi	Another term for vegetables
Simmer	Heating food just below boiling level

Upma	A light snack prepared with semolina or vermicelli
Uthappam	A thick pancake made of fermented batter with or without vegetables
Vada	A ring shaped snack made of fermented gram flour batter and deep fried in oil to crispy form

Language guide
This table will help you to know all about the various food items in nine major languages of India.

Cereals

English	Hindi	Bengali	Oriya	Marathi	Gujarati
Barley	Jau	Job	Jabadhana	Barley	Barley
Millet	Bajra	Bajra	Bajra	Bajri	Bajri
Milo	Juar	Juar	Janha	Jwari	Juwar
Maize	Bhutta	Bhutta	Sukhila maka	Maka	Makai
Rice	Chawal	Chowl	Chaula	Tandool	Chokha
Rice boiled	Usna chawal	Sidha chowl	Usuna chaula	Ukda tandool	Ukra chokha
Rice pressed	Chudwa	Chira	Chuda	Pohe	Pohwa
Rice puffed	Murmara	Mudi	Mudhi	Murmere	Mumra
Ragi	Makra	Madua	Mandia	Nachni	Ragi
Semolina	Sooji	Sooji	Sooji	Rava	Rava
Vermicelli	Siwain	Semai	Simai	Shevaya	Sev
Wheat	Gehu	Gom	Gahama	Gahu	Ghau

Pulses

English	Hindi	Bengali	Oriya	Marathi	Gujarati
Bengal gram whole	Chana	Chola	Buta	Harbara	Channi
Bengal gram split	Chana dal	Cholardal	Butar dali	Harbar dal	Channa dal
Black gram	Urad dal	Mashkalaidal	Biri	Uddachi dal	Alad
Green gram whole	Moong	Moong	Mooga	Moong	Moog
Green gram split	Moong dal	Moongdal	Mooga dali	Moongachi dal	Moog ni dal
Horse gram	Kulthi	Kulthikalai	Kolatha	Kuleeth	Kuleeth
Kidney beans	Rajmah	Rajmah	Rajmah	Shravan	Phanasi
Peas	Mattar	Matar	Matara	Vatana	Suka vatana
Red gram	Turdal	Arhardal	Harada	Tur dal	Tuverni dal

Flour and powders					
English	Hindi	Bengali	Oriya	Marathi	Gujarati
Bengal gram	Besan	Besan	Besana	Besan	Besan
Refined flour	Maida	Maida	Maida	Maida	Maida
Mango powder	Amchur	Aamer guda	Sukila amba gunda	Amchur	Karino powder
Wheat flour	Aata	Aata	Atta	Kaneek	Ato

Spices and condiments					
English	Hindi	Bengali	Oriya	Marathi	Gujarati
Asafoetida	Hing	Hing	Hingu	HIng	Hing
Bay leaf	Tej pattha	Tej paata	Tej patra	Tamal patra	Tamal patra
Cardamom	Elaichi	Elaich	Alaicha	Veldoda	Elaichi
Cloves	Lavang	Labang	Labanga	Lavang	Lavang
Cinnamon	Dalchini	Dalchini	Dalchini	Dalchini	Tuj
Coriander	Dhaniya	Dhanai	Dhania	Dhane	Dhania
Coconut	Copra	Narkel	Nadiya	Naral	Naliyer
Cumin	Jeera	Jeere	Jeera	Jeera	Jeeru
Fenugreek	Methi	Methi	Methi	Methi	Methi
Gingely seed	Til	Til	Rasi	Til	Tal
Ground nuts	Mungphalli	China badam	China badam	Bhui moong	Bhoising
Garlic	Lahsun	Rashun	Rasuna	Lasoon	Lasan
Ginger	Adhrak	Aada	Ada	Ale	Adu
Mace	Javithri	Jayitri	Jayitri	Jaypatri	Jaypatri
Mustard seed	Rai	Sorse	Sorisa	Mohori	Rai
Nutmeg	Jaiphal	Jaiphal	Jaiphal	Jaiphal	Jaiphal
Oregano	Ajwain	Joan	Juani	Onva	Oregano
Pepper	Kalimirch	Golmarich	Golmaricha	Mire	Mari
Poppy seed	Khus khus	Posto	Posto	Khus khus	Khus Khus
Red chilly	Lal mirchi	Lal lanka	Lali lanka	Mirch	Mirch
Tamarind	Imli	Tetul	Tentuli	Chinch	Amli
Turmeric	Haldi	Holud	Haldi	Halad	Haldhar

Nuts and other items					
English	Hindi	Bengali	Oriya	Marathi	Gujarati
Almond	Badam	Badam	Badama	Badam	Badam
Black salt	Kala namak	Kala laban	Saindha laban	Black salt	Black salt
Borneol	Borneol	Borneol	Borneol	Borneol	Borneol
Citric acid	Citric acid	Citric acid	Citric acid	Citric acid	Citric acid
Cashew	Kaju	Hijlibadam	Lankamba manji	Kaju	Kaju
Honey	Shahad	Mou	Mohu	Madh	Honey
Jaggery	Gud	Gud	Guda	Gul	Gol
Pistachios	Pista	Pesta	Pista	Pista	Pista

Raisin	Kismish	Kismish	Kismish	Bedane	Lal draksh
Sugar	Chini	Chini	Chini	Sugar	Sugar
Walnut	Akhrot	Akrot	Akhroot	Akrod	Akrot

Oil and clarifiers

English	Hindi	Bengali	Oriya	Marathi	Gujarati
Butter	Makkhan	Makhan	Lohuni	Lonee	Makhan
Ghee	Ghee	Ghee	Gheeya	Thup	Ghee
Oil	Thel	Thel	Tela	Thel	Thel

Liquids and solids

English	Hindi	Bengali	Oriya	Marathi	Gujarati
Buttermilk	Lassi	Ghol doyi	Ghola dahi	Tak	Chhas
Cream	Malai	Sar	Sara	Cream	Cream
Curd	Dahi	Doyi	Dahi	Dahi	Dahi
Cheese	Paneer	Chhana	Chhena	Paneer	Paneer
Khoa	Khoa	Khoa	Khua	Khava	Khoa
Milk	Doodh	Doodh	Dudha	Doodh	Doodh

Vegetables

English	Hindi	Bengali	Oriya	Marathi	Gujarati
Ash gourd	Petha	Chalkumra	Pani kakharu	Kohala	Safed koloo
Beetroot	Chukandar	Beetroot	Bita	Beet	Beet
Bottle gourd	Lauki	Lau	Lau	Pandhara bhopla	Doodhi
Bitter gourd	Karela	Karala	Kalara	Karle	Karela
Brinjal	Baingan	Begun	Baigana	Vangi	Ringena
Beans broad	Bakla	Makhan sim	Simba	Ghewda	Papdi
Carrot	Gajar	Gajar	Gajara	Gajar	Gajar
Carissa	Carissa	Carissa	Carissa	Carissa	Carissa
Colocasia	Arvi	Kochu	Saru	Alu kanda	Alvi
Cabbage	Bandh gobi	Badha kopi	Bandha kobi	Kobi	Kobi
Capsicum	Simla mirch	Simla lanka	Simla lanka	Bhopli mirchi	Simla marchan
Cauliflower	Phool gobi	Pool kopi	Phool kobi	Phool khobi	Phool khobi
Cluster beans	Guer ki phalli	Jhar sim	Guanara chhuin	Govar	Govar
Coconut	Nariyal	Narkel	Nadiya	Naral	Naliyer
Cucumber	Khira	Sasha	Kakudi	Kakadi	Kakadi
Drumstick	Sajan ki phalli	Sajana danta	Sajna chhuin	Shevaga sheng	Saragavo
French beans	Bakla	Beans	Beans	Pharas bee	Fansi
Gerkin	Tindli	Telakuch	Kundru	Tondale	Tondale
Jackfruit	Kathal	Kanthal	Panasa katha	Phanas	Kawla phanas
Lemon	Nimbu	Lebu	Lembu	Limbu	Kadgi limbu

English	Hindi	Bengali	Oriya	Marathi	Gujarati
Ladies finger	Bhendi	Dharash	Bhendi	Bhendi	Bhinda
Mango	Aam	Kancha aam	Kanch amba	Kairi	Keri
Mango ginger	Haldi aam	Amada	Amba ada	Amba haldi	Amba haldi
Onion	Pyaz	Pyaz	Pyaza	Kanda	Kanda
Onion madras	Madras pyaz	Madras pyaz	Madras pyaza	Madras pyaz	Madras pyaz
Peas	Mattar	Mattar	Matara	Vatana	Vatana
Potato	Alu	Gol alu	Alu	Batata	Batata
Plantain green	Kela	Kanch kala	Bantala kadali	Kele	Kela
Plantain flower	Kele ka phool	Mocha	Kadali bhanda	Kel phool	Kel phool
Plantain stem	Kele ka tana	Thor	Kdali manja	Kelicha khunt	Kelanu thed
Pumpkin	Kaddu	Kumra	Kakharu	Lal bhopla	Kohlu
Radish	Mooli	Moola	Moola	Mooli	Mooli
Ridge gourd	Turai	Jhinga	Janhi	Dodka	Turia
Snake gourd	Chachinda	Chichinga	Chachindia	Padval	Pandola
Sweet potato	Shakkarkand	Ranga alu	Kanda mula	Ratala	Sakkaria
Tomato	Tamatar	Bilati begun	Bilati baigana	Tomato	Tamatu
Yam	Ratula	Khaam alu	Khamba alu	Goradu	Ratalu

Green vegetables

English	Hindi	Bengali	Oriya	Marathi	Gujarati
Amaranthus leaf	Chauli sag	Notya	Notya saag	Math	Choli ni bhaji
Basella leaf	Besella leaf	Basella leaf	Basella leaf	Basella leaf	Basella leaf
Cannabinus	Cannabinus	Cannabinus	Cannabinus	Cannabinus	Cannabinus
Chuka leaf	Chuka	Chuka palang	Chuka saga	Ambat chuka	Chuka ni bhaji
Colocasia leaf	Arvi ka sag	Kochu saag	Searu patra	Alupan	Alu na patra
Coriander leaf	Hara dhania	Dhane paata	Dhania patra	Kothimbir	Kothmir
Curry leaf	Kadi pattha	Bhursunga	Bursunga patra	Kadhi limb	Mitho limbdo
Drumstick leaf	Sajjan pattha	Sajna saag	Sajna saga	Shevaga pan	Seragvani Bhaji
Fenugreek leaf	Methi saag	Methi saag	Methi saga	Methi bhaji	Methi Bhaji
Mint leaf	Pudina	Pudina	Pudina patra	Pudina	Pudina
Mustard leaf	Sarson ka saag	Sorse saag	Sorisa saga	Moharicha pan	Rai ni Bhaji
Radish leaf	Mooli ka saag	Mular saag	Mula saga	Mooli pan	Mooli na patra

| Spinach | Palak | Palang saag | Palanga saga | Palak | Palak |
| Tamarind leaf | Imli ka pattha | Tetul patta | Tentuli patra | Chinchecha pala | Amli na patra |

Fruits

English	Hindi	Bengali	Oriya	Marathi	Gujarati
Apple	Sev	Aapel	Seu	Sufarchand	Safarjan
Apricot	Khoobani	Apricot	Apricot	Apricot	Apricot
Banana	Kela	Kala	Chamapa kadali	Kela	Kela
Black plum	Kala Jamun	Kalajam	Jamukoli	Jambhool	Jambu
Chikku	Sapota	Chiku	Sapota	Chikku	Chikku
Custard apple	Seethaphal	Aat	Aaita	Sitaphal	Sitaphal
Dates	Khajur	Khejur	Khajura	Khajur	Khajur
Figs	Anjeer	Dumoor	Dimiri	Anjeer	Anjeer
Grapes	Angoor	Angoor	Angoora	Draksha	Draksha
Gauva	Amrud	Piyara	Pijuli	Peru	Jamphal
Jack fruit	Kathal	Kanthal	Panasa	Phanas	Phanas
Mango	Aam	Aam	Amba	Amba	Keri
Orange	Santra	Kamala	Kamala	Santre	Santra
Papaya	Papita	Pepe	Amrut bhanda	Popai	Papaya
Pineapple	Ananas	Anarash	Sapuri	Ananas	Ananas
Pears	Nashpati	Nashpati	Nashpati	Nashpati	Nasapatti
Plum	Alubhukara	Plum	Plum	Plum	Plum
Pomegranate	Anar	Dalim	Dalimba	Dalimb	Dalamb
Sweet lime	Mousambi	Mousambi	Mousambi	Mausambi	Mausambi
Water melon	Tarbhooj	Tarmuj	Tarmuja	Kharbooja	Kharbooja
Wood apple	Kaith	Kothbel	Kaitha	Kavith	Kothu

Conversions

Abbreviations

tsp	teaspoon
tbsp	tablespoon
oz	ounce
gm	gram
cm	centimetre
ml	millilitre

Temperatures

Fahrenheit	Celsius
350	175
375	190
400	205
425	220
450	230

Volume

1/8 tsp	1/2 ml
1/4 tsp	1 ml
1/2 tsp	2 ml
1 tsp	5 ml
2 tsp	10 ml
1 tbsp	15 ml
1/4 cup (4 tbsp)	60 ml
1/3 cup	80 ml
1/2 cup	120 ml
2/3 cup	160 ml
3/4 cup	180 ml
1 cup	240 ml
4 cups (1 quart)	940 ml
4 1/4 cup	1 litre

Weights

1 oz	28 gm
2 oz	57 gm
4 oz (1/4 lb)	114 gm
6 oz	170 gm
8 oz (1/2 lb)	227 gm
12 oz	340 gm
16 oz (1 lb)	454 gm
32 oz (2 lb)	908 gm
2.2 lb	1 kg

Linear measurements

1/2 inch	1 cm
1 inch	2.5 cm
6 inches	15 cm
8 inches	20 cm

THE BASICS

Ghee

1 Cup of butter

Melt the butter in a small heavy bottomed saucepan on low heat. Increase the heat to simmer and let it brown, about 10 minutes or so, or until the milk solids on the bottom of the pan will start to brown. Do not let them burn.

Remove from the heat and cool. Skim the foam from the surface and carefully drain the ghee into a glass jar, leaving the solids behind. Use in recipes and store rest in refrigerator for later use.

Garam Masala

Ingredients

Cinnamon Sticks 5 (3 in.) sticks
cardamom pods 1 cup
cumin seeds 1/2 cup
black pepper 1/2 cup
cloves 1/2 cup
coriander seeds 1/2 cup
Coconut - grated (opt.) 1/4 cup

Preparation

Dry the ingredients in an oven. Do not let them turn brown. Remove the seeds from the cardamom pods. Pound cinnamon sticks into smaller size. Combine ingredients until they are well mixed and blend at high speed for 2 or 3 min's. Till completely pulverized.

CHUTNEY

Chutneys

India is famous for its chutneys. A chutney is a fresh or cooked relish from the cuisine of India. It is usually eaten in small amounts to add flavour and to accent a meal. A fresh chutney in India is customarily ground fresh on grinding stone and is made fresh daily. It is made of peanuts, cashews, fresh herbs, fresh chillies, ginger, garlic and fresh green mangoes or lime juice with spices. Fresh chutneys are very refreshing. Cooked chutneys are made seasonally using fruits like tomatoes, mangoes, pineapples, tamarind, apples, pears that are combined with fresh seasonings like ginger, hot chillies and lemon juice and cooked with spices to create heavenly concoction of tastes.

Coconut Chutney - North Indian (fresh)

Ingredients:
3 tbsp. coconut, shredded
1 inch fresh ginger, chopped
1 fresh green chilli
1/2 bunch cilantro with stems and root removed
fresh lemon juice
salt to taste

Method:
In a food processor or blender add all ingredients into a pesto like sauce.

Coconut Chutney (Thengai Thigayal) - South Indian (fresh)

Ingredients:
1 cup fresh coconut, shredded
1/2 cup Toor dal dry
1/4 cup Urad dal dry
1/4 cup Channa dal dry
1/4 tsp tamarind concentrate
1/4 tsp. asafoetida
Whole red chillies as per taste up to 3
Salt to taste
2 tsp. cooking oil

Method:
Dry roast toor dhal, chana dhal, urad dhal, red chillies and asafoetida in cooking oil. Grind this mixture in water into a thick paste. Add coconut, tamarind and salt and grind it for a few more seconds until all the mixture blends into a smooth paste. Serve with steamed rice or can be served with dosa (rice pancakes).

Tamarind Chutney (cooked)

Ingredients:
1 cup cleaned tamarind
1/2 cup dates deseeded
1/4 cup sugar
2 cups water
1/2 tsp. red chilli powder
1/2 crushed cumin seeds
1 tsp. salt
3/4 cup jaggery

Method:
Wash the tamarind clean.
Place the tamarind, jaggery, sugar, dates and water in a deep boiling pan.
Soak for a few minutes. Put to boil for about 7-8 minutes.
Cool to room temperature. Blend in a electric blender till smooth.
Strain and transfer to the pan again. Boil till thick enough to coat the back of a spoon thinly.
Add the seasoning. Cool again. Store in clean airtight bottles and refrigerate.

Tomato Chutney (cooked)

Ingredients:
2 Tbsp. Ghee
1/4 tsp. red chillies
1 tsp. cumin seeds
1 inch ginger minced
1 inch of cinnamon stick
2 cups coarsely fresh ripe tomatoes
3 Tbsp. jaggery or brown sugar
Salt to taste

Method:
Heat ghee in a large sauce pan over moderate heat. Add the cumin seeds and let sizzle and brown. Add red chillies, ginger and stir fry for a moment. Add the other ingredients. Cook on low for about 20 to 35 minutes. Serve with meals.

Cashew Nut Chutney (fresh)

Ingredients: -
prep time 10 minutes makes a little over 1 cup
1 cup raw cashews bits or halves
1/4 tsp. lemon juice
1 teaspoon salt
1/2-inch piece of peeled fresh ginger root, sliced
1-2 hot green chillies,
Seeded and chopped up to 1/3 cups water
2 tablespoons chopped fresh coriander

Method: Combine the cashews, lemon juice, salt ginger and chillies 1/4 of cup water in a food processor fitted with the metal blade, or a blender, and process until smooth, adding more water as necessary to produce a loose puree. Transfer to a bowl, add the fresh coriander, and serve or cover well and keep refrigerated for up to 3 days. Note: This chutney thickens as it sits. Thin it with water to the desired consistency.

Cilantro Chutney (fresh)

Ingredients:
1 bunch cilantro, fresh
1 or 2 small seedless green chilli, fresh,
juice of one lime
salt to taste
1/2 teaspoon cumin seeds, roasted, ground
1 pinch of black pepper
1 tbsp. coriander powder

Method:
Dry roast cumin seeds in a hot cast iron frying pan, until they turn brown.
Grind into powder.
Put all the ingredients into the blender and puree into a paste.
Use as little water as necessary.

Mango Chutney

1/4 cup refined oil
1 teaspoon mustard seeds
1/2 teaspoon turmeric powder
1 1/2 kg. Raw mango
1/2 teaspoon salt
1 cup water,
5 cups sugar

Directions:
Skin the mangoes. Remove the seeds and cut the mangoes into small pieces. Keep them aside.
Heat the oil in a pan. Sprinkle the mustard seeds into the oil.
Just as the seeds start to crack, add the turmeric powder, salt and mango pieces into the pan.

Stir them thoroughly and add the water. Allow the whole thing to come to a boil. Add sugar to it and continue boiling. The chutney will be thickening. In the process continuous stirring is a must. When the chutney becomes thick remove the pan from burner. Let it cool to normal temperature. Refrigerate and serve cold.

Coconut Chutney

Ingredients

Coconut (grated) 1 cup
Chana Daal 2 tsp.
Green Chilli 2 - 3
Ginger 1 inch

Coriander Leaves
Hing 1/4 tsp.
Lemon Juice to taste
Salt to taste

Preparation

- Fry Chana Daal (if used).
- Grind all ingredients and mix.
- It's also possible to use yogurt, in which case the Lemon juice may be left out. Or used. Anything goes, apparently.

Zucchini Chutney

Ingredients

Zucchini 2-3
Onions 1
Hing 1/2 tsp.
Tamcon 1/2 tsp.
Green chillies 2-3

Preparation

- Fry cut zucchini, onions, and green chillies.
- Add turmeric, salt, cook on low flame for 5 - 10 minutes.
- Boil tamcon, add to mix above.
- Pulverize the whole thing in blender.
- Seasoning: Thalshi Kottify with mustard seeds, urad daal.

Lemon Pickle

Ingredients

Lemons 6
Salt 5 tsp.
Chilli powder 5 tsp.
Turmeric pinch
Hing 1 tsp.
Methi 1 tsp.
Oil 5 tbsp.

Preparation

- Cut lemons into small pieces and remove the seeds. Add salt and keep for about 12 hours.
- Add chilli powder, turmeric, and methi.
- Heat oil, mustard seeds, and asafoetida. Spread this mixture over the lemons.
- Mix thoroughly.

RICE

BOILED RICE

Ingredients
Rice   500 gm
Salt   to taste

Method:

- Pick, wash and soak rice.
- Bring water to boil
- Add rice, salt and simmer
- When rice is cooked, drain water and serve hot.

STEAMED RICE

Ingredients
Rice   500 gm
Bay leaf   5 gm
Cinnamon   5 gm
Fat   50 gm
Cardamom   5 gm
Cloves   5 gm
Salt   to taste

Method:

- Wash and clean rice, soak it.
- Heat fat, add whole spices and rice. Fry.
- Add water to rice in 2:1 ratio. Add salt and cook
- Finish cooking in oven.
- Serve hot.

Lemon Rice

Ingredients

Rice 1 cup
Oil 2 tbsp.
Mustard Seeds 1 tsp.
Urad Daal 1 tsp.
Chana Daal 1 tsp.
Cashews handful
Raisins handful
Turmeric pinch
mixed vegetables. 1 cup
Lemon 1

Preparation

- Cook rice.
- Heat oil and add all other ingredients except for the lemon. Fry as appropriate.
- Mix stuff in pan with rice. Squeeze the lemon and add the juice to the rice.

Tomato Rice

Ingredients

Rice 1 cup
Tomatoes 1/2 can
Green Pepper 1
Onions 1-2
Green Chillies 2-3
Ginger 1/2 inch
Garlic 2-3 cloves
Fresh coriander bunch
Random spices

Preparation

- Fry cut onions, green pepper, ginger, garlic, random spices (cloves, black pepper, cinnamon, cardamom, bay leaves) and salt for 5 - 10 minutes.
- Add tomatoes, sauté for a while.
- Add washed and drained rice, fry for 5 minutes or so. Add more water and cook until rice is done.

- **Extra fancy:** Top rice with cheese, tomato and green pepper slices (rings, e.g.) and bake for 20 - 25 minutes at 250o.

CURD RICE

INGREDIENTS

Ingredients
Rice	400 gm
Fresh curd	600 ml
Milk	400 ml
Salt	to taste
Ginger	10 gm
Green Chillies	10 gm
Mustard seeds	4 gm
Asafoetida	A pinch
Curry leaves	1 sprig
Oil	30 ml

METHOD

- Boil rice, add salt and cook slightly
- Mix with curd, add boiled and cooked milk chop green chillies and ginger
- Heat oil, fry mustered seed and asafoetida.
- Add curry leaves and chopped ingredients sauté for 2 minutes.
- Switch off the fire and add the rice, curd mixture to the pan
- Mix well
- Serve with pickles

Plain Savoury Rice - Namkin Chawal

Ingredients:
Serves: 4
21/2 cups long grain rice
4 cups hot water
2 teaspoons ghee
2 1/2 teaspoons salt

Method:
Wash rice well and soak I hour in cold water. Drain in colander while bringing water, ghee and salt to the boil in a heavy saucepan with a well-fitting lid. Add rice, stir and bring quickly to the boil. Turn heat very low, cover tightly and cook, without lifting lid or stirring, for 20-25 minutes. Lift lid to allow steam to escape for about 5 minutes, and then lightly fluff up rice with fork, taking care not to mash the grains, which will be firm, separate and perfectly cooked. Dish up using a slotted metal spoon rather than a wooden spoon, which will crush the grains. Serve with curries or other spiced dishes.

Festive Spiced Rice - Rajasthani Pilau

The State of Rajasthan is beautiful. Costumes in vivid colours dazzle and enchant. Even the food reflects this love of colour, dishes being garnished with the bright reds and greens that Rajasthani folk delight in.

Ingredients:
Serves: 4-6
2 1/2 cups long grain rice
3 tablespoons ghee or oil
2 medium onions, finely sliced
2 sticks cinnamon
6 cardamom pods, bruised
6 whole cloves
10 whole black pepper
4 cups hot stock or water
Salt to taste

Method:
If the rice needs washing, wash well in several changes of cold water and leave to soak for 1 hour. Then drain in a colander for at least 30 minutes.
Heat ghee or oil in a large, heavy saucepan and fry the sliced onion with the cinnamon, cardamoms, black pepper and cloves until the onions are golden, stirring frequently so that they brown evenly. Add the rice and fry for about 3 minutes, then pour in the stock or water. Add the salt and stir well while bringing quickly to the boil. Turn heat very low, cover tightly and cook without lifting lid for 25 minutes. Uncover, allow steam to escape for a few minutes, remove whole spices.
Serve hot with curry.

Rice with Peas - Mattar Pilau   (Uttar Pradesh)

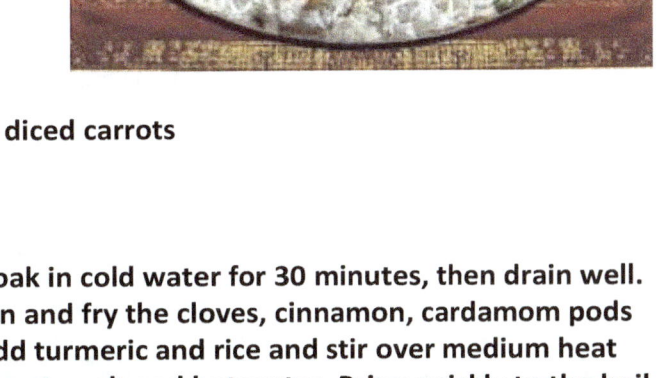

Ingredients:
Serves: 4-5
1 1/2 cups long grain rice
1 tablespoon ghee
4 whole cloves
1 small cinnamon stick
3 or 4 cardamom pods, bruised
1 teaspoon cumin seeds
1/2 teaspoon ground turmeric
1 1/2cups shelled green peas and diced carrots
2 1/2 teaspoons salt
3 1/4 cups hot water

Wash the rice well and leave to soak in cold water for 30 minutes, then drain well. Heat the ghee in a heavy saucepan and fry the cloves, cinnamon, cardamom pods and cumin seeds, for 1 minute. Add turmeric and rice and stir over medium heat for about 3 minutes. Add peas/carrots, salt and hot water. Bring quickly to the boil, then turn heat very low, cover with a well-fitting lid and cook for 25-30 minutes without lifting lid or stirring. Uncover at end of cooking time to allow steam to escape for about 3 minutes. Remove whole spices, fork rice grains lightly and serve hot with meat or vegetable curries.

Rice with Sesame Seeds - Til Bhath

Ingredients:
Serves: 4-6
2'h cups long grain rice
4 cups water
2'/s teaspoons salt
2 tablespoons light sesame oil
1 teaspoon mustard seeds
12 curry leaves
1 cup sesame seeds lemon juice to taste
Method:
Put rice, water and salt into a heavy saucepan, bring to the boil. Cover with well-fitting lid, turn heat very low and cook for 20 minutes. Turn off heat and leave while preparing seasoning.

Heat Sesame Oil in small saucepan and fry the mustard seeds and curry leaves until leaves are brown and Mustard Seeds pop. Add the sesame seeds and keep stirring over medium heat until the seeds are evenly golden brown. Mix this seasoning together with the hot cooked rice and add a little lemon juice to taste. Serve with curried vegetables, fresh chutney and fried pappadoms.

Spicy Rice Maharashtrian Style - Masala Bhath - (Maharashtra)

Ingredients:
Serves: 6
3 cups long grain rice
3 tablespoons ghee
3 tablespoons oil
3 large onions, finely sliced
5 cardamom pods, bruised
2 small sticks cinnamon
6 whole cloves
20 whole black peppercorns
1/2 teaspoon ground turmeric
5 cups hot water
3 teaspoons salt
1/2 cup raw peanuts/cashew nuts, split in halves
2 sprigs fresh curry leaves or 20 dried curry leaves
3 fresh green chillies, seeded and sliced
2 teaspoons black mustard seeds

Method:
Wash rice well and leave to drain in colander for at least 30 minutes. In a large, heavy saucepan heat half the ghee and oil and fry the onions and whole spices until onions are golden brown, stirring frequently. Remove half the onions and set aside for garnish. Add turmeric and rice to pan and fry, stirring with slotted metal spoon, until all the grains are coated with the ghee. Add the hot water and salt, stir well and bring to the boil. Cover with tightly fitting lid and turn heat very low. Cook for 20-25 minutes without lifting lid.

Heat remaining ghee and oil in a small pan and fry the peanuts/cashew nuts until golden. Remove with slotted spoon. Fry the curry leaves, green chillies and mustard seeds until the seeds pop. Pour over the rice, lightly fork through. Dish up rice and garnish with the fried cashews, chopped coriander leaves and grated fresh coconut.

Rice with Yogurt   - Thair Sadam

In southern: India, this dish is often served as the finale to a festive meal, but it may be presented as the meal itself, accompanied by curries and pickles.

Ingredients:
Serves: 4-6
2 1/2 cups long grain rice
4 cups water
Salt to taste
2 tablespoons ghee or oil
1 teaspoon black cumin seeds
1 teaspoon black mustard seeds
1 teaspoon urad dhal
1/4 teaspoon asafoetida, optional
3 fresh red or green chillies, seeded and sliced
3 cups yogurt
salt to taste

Method:
Put well washed and drained rice into a saucepan with the water and salt. Bring quickly to the boil, then cover tightly, turn heat very low and cook for 20 minutes without lifting lid.

In another pan heat the ghee and fry the black cumin, mustard, dhal, asafoetida (if used) and chillies until the mustard seeds pop and the dhal is golden brown. Remove from heat, garnish into the yogurt and add a little salt to taste. Mix thoroughly with the cooked rice.

Rice in Coconut Milk - Nariyal Bhath

Ingredients:
Serves: 6
2 1/2 cups long grain rice
2 tablespoons ghee
2 medium onions, finely sliced
10 curry leaves
10 whole black peppercorns
1 small stick cinnamon
6 cardamom pods, bruised
6 whole cloves
a few cashew nuts
3/4 teaspoon ground turmeric

4 cups coconut milk
2 1/2 teaspoons salt
Garnish:
1/2 cup fried cashew nuts

Method:
Wash rice and drain for at least 30 minutes. Heat the ghee in a heavy saucepan and fry the onions, curry leaves and whole spices, cashew nuts, stirring frequently, until the onions are golden. Add the turmeric and the rice and fry, stirring, until the rice is coated with the ghee, about 3 or 4 minutes. Add the coconut milk and salt, stir and bring to the boil, then cover with a well-fitting lid, turn heat very low and cook for 25 minutes or until the coconut milk is absorbed.

Serve the rice hot, garnished with fried cashews and accompanied by curries and sambals.

Saffron Pilaf - (Zaffarani Pulao)

Ingredients:

2 cups long grain rice, preferably Basmati
3 to 4 fresh ripe peaches, or 1 (16 oz.) can peaches in syrup, drained
6 tablespoons ghee or vegetable oil
1/4 cup slivered blanched almonds
1/4 cup unsalted pistachios
1 medium onion, finely chopped
1 (3.inch long) cinnamon stick
1 cup milk
1/4 cup seedless raisins
1/2 teaspoon ground cardamom
1/2 teaspoon powdered saffron
Salt, to taste

Directions:
Soak the rice in 3 cups cold water for 30 minutes. Drain the rice, reserving the water, and set aside. Cut the peaches lengthwise into 1/2.inch slices. Heat the ghee or oil in a large saucepan over moderate heat and sauté the peach slices until golden on both sides, 3 to 4 minutes. Remove with a slotted spoon and drain on paper towels.

In the same ghee, sauté the almonds until golden brown, about 2 minutes. Remove and drain. Repeat with the pistachios. Set the almonds and pistachios aside. Add the onion to the ghee remaining in the pan and sauté until tender, about 3 minutes. Add the cinnamon stick and fry for 1 minute. Add the rice and stir constantly for 2 minutes, until the rice begins to brown and is thoroughly coated with the ghee. Add the reserved water, milk, raisins, cardamom, saffron and salt.

Bring to a boil, stirring occasionally to prevent the rice from sticking to the bottom of the pan. Reduce the heat to low and simmer covered for 10 minutes. Remove from the heat and allow to sit covered for 15 minutes. Fluff the rice with a fork, remove and discard the cinnamon stick, and transfer to a serving platter. Surround the rice with the reserved peach slices and sprinkle with the almonds and pistachios.

Raita and Pachchadi

Raitas and pachchadis based on yogurt to act as coolers in contrast to the hot and spicy chutneys that dot the Indian meal. All the recipes below serve 4 to 6 .

Yogurt with Cucumbers (Punjab - North India)

Ingredients:
2 green cucumbers
Salt and black pepper to taste
2 tablespoons finely chopped spring onion
2 cups yogurt
1'/2 teaspoons roasted cumin seeds (optional)
Garnish:
1 tablespoon chopped fresh coriander or mint

Method:
Peel the cucumbers, halve them lengthways and remove the seeds. Cut the cucumbers into small dice, sprinkle with salt and leave for 15 minutes, then drain away liquid and rinse the cucumbers quickly in cold water. Drain well. Combine with onion, yogurt, lemon juice and taste to see if more salt is required. Roast the cumin seeds in a dry pan, shaking pan or stirring constantly, until brown. Bruise or crush seeds and sprinkle over yogurt. Serve chilled, garnished with mint or coriander.

Palak Pachchadi

Ingredients:
1 large bunch spinach 2 teaspoons ghee or oil
1 teaspoon black mustard seeds
l teaspoon cumin seeds
1 teaspoon ground cumin
1/2 teaspoon fenugreek seeds
1/8 teaspoon chilli powder (optional)
Salt and black pepper to taste
2 cups yogurt

Method:
1. Wash spinach thoroughly in several changes of water. Remove any tough stems and put the leaves into a saucepan with very little water. Cover and steam over low heat until spinach is tender. Drain and chop finely.
2. In a small pan heat ghee or oil and fry the mustard seeds until they start to pop. Add cumin seeds, ground cumin and fenugreek seeds and continue to fry, stirring with a wooden spoon, until the fenugreek seeds are golden brown, but do not allow to burn. Remove from heat, stir in chilli powder, if used, and salt and allow to cool. Mix in the yogurt, then stir this mixture into the spinach. Serve cold or at room temperature as a side dish with rice and curry, or with one of the Indian breads.

Yogurt and Onion Salad - Dahi Kachumbar - (Maharashtra)

Ingredients:
3 medium onions
Salt and black pepper to taste
1 cup yogurt
1 teaspoon finely grated fresh ginger
2 medium tomatoes, peeled and chopped
3 fresh green chillies, seeded and chopped
3 tablespoons chopped fresh cilantro or coriander

Method:
Cut the onions into thin slices, sprinkle with the salt and set aside for 20 minutes. Squeeze out as much liquid as possible. Mix together the yogurt and ginger, then fold in the onions and the rest of the ingredients. Cover and chill thoroughly before serving.

Yogurt with Bananas - Kela Raita

Ingredients:
4 large ripe bananas lemon juice
1 teaspoon cumin seeds
1 cup yogurt
3 tablespoons freshly grated or desiccated coconut
1/2 teaspoon salt
2 teaspoons sugar

Method:
Slice the bananas and sprinkle with lemon juice. Roast cumin seeds in a dry pan, shaking or stirring constantly until brown. Crush or grind. Combine the yogurt with all the ingredients except the banana. If desiccated coconut is used, moisten it first by sprinkling with about 2 tablespoons water and tossing it with the fingers until it is no longer dry. Fold banana into yogurt mixture. Chill and serve.

Onion, Tomato & Cucumber Raita

Ingredients:

2 cups yogurt/curds
Cilantro/coriander leaves
1 small onion, chopped fine
1 small cucumber, grated
1 small tomato, chopped fine
1 tsp. oil
1 tsp. mustard seeds
Salt and pepper to taste

Directions:
Mix the yogurt/curds, onions and tomatoes, cilantro/ coriander leaves, cucumber, salt and pepper. Fry the mustard seeds in oil and add to the mixture. Serve.

BREADS

Flat Breads

Indian daily breads are called chapatti, phulka and roti and paratha. They are made of finely milled whole wheat flour and water. Some recipes call for salt or oil but I like to make mine without them. The cooks that use salt and oil say it tenderizes the dough. For me the taste of salt and oil in Indian bread dough interferes with the overall meal as the bread does not stay neutral/innocent in taste. Pooris are fried breads that are usually made on holidays, festive occasions and for entertaining. Indian flat breads are used to scoop up curries and vegetables.

Tools required for making Indian Flatbreads

Cast Iron concave griddle 8-12 inches in diameter called tawa
a shallow mixing bowl
A rolling pin
a large plate for dusting the dough while rolling it out
tongs for the beginner
wok stand placed over the electric or gas burner
a grilling rack which is placed over the wok stand
a wok for deep frying for Pooris and other fried breads only

Making dough for Indian Flatbreads

Put flour in a large bowl. Make a well in the middle and pour in a stream of water in the centre. Use one hand to mix the flour and water in a rotating motion from the centre of the bowl outward, until the dough is moist enough to be gathered into a rough mass. Wet hands and continue until the mixture cleans the sides of the bowl and has become a non-stick, kneadable dough. When the dough is kneaded, it will be elastic and silky smooth. To test the dough, press it lightly with a fingertip. If it springs back, it is ready to be rested. Resting the dough is the last step and allows the dough to relax and absorb the water and kneading. Rest for 1/2 hour in warm climates and 1.5 hours in cold climates. Cover with a wet towel so the dough does not dry out. The rested dough is light and springy, less resistant to being rolled out into the thin rounds.
I like to mix, knead, rest and then refrigerated for convenience and use daily. My dough lasts in the refrigerator for about 5 days. It also makes rolling out easier than the freshly made dough.

Roti/Chapatti

Once you taste these unleavened, unsalted simple breads - a person is hooked. This is simple, unpretentious home cooking but very satisfying, healthy and easy on the pocket book. There are also excellent for those with a yeast allergy. Rotis are made from small balls of dough that are rolled out and then partially cooked on a hot griddle and then finished directly over high heat. The high heat makes the rotis puff up into a ball. They are then lightly coated with ghee to keep them pliable until serving time. Line a tortilla basket with a napkin and keep the rotis in it. Allow 2-3 chapattis or rotis per person. This is everyday Indian bread made in most Indian homes daily.

Ingredients to make about 6:
2.5 cups chapatti flour
1 cup water at room temperature
1 cup chapatti flour
ghee,

Method to roll out the dough:
Prepare the desired amount of dough from the Basic Dough recipe. After resting for 2-2 1/2 hours, knead well. Divide the dough into peach-size balls. On a lightly floured surface, flatten one ball of dough with your hand. Using a rolling-pin, roll out the dough into a thin, round patty, about 5 inches in diameter. Roll from the centre, turning patty several times to prevent sticking. Try to make the edges slightly thinner than the centre. As you cook the chapatti/roti, one could be rolling out the next, rather than shaping all of the chapattis at one time.

Method of cooking the chapatti or roti:
Preheat a cast-iron tawa over medium heat. Place the rolled dough on the palm of one hand and flip it over on to the tawa. When the colour changes on the top and bubbles appear, turn it over. When both sides are done, use kitchen tongs (chimta) to remove the chapatti from the skillet.
Gas Stove: If you have a gas stove, hold the cooked chapatti over a medium flame and it will puff up immediately. Turn quickly to flame-bake the other side. Do this several times, taking care that the edges are well cooked.
Electric Stove: If you have an electric stove, chapattis can be encouraged to puff by pressing them with a clean kitchen towel after the first turn on each side. Repeat the shaping and cooking process until all chapattis are cooked.
To keep the chapattis warm as they are cooked, place them in a towel-lined bowl and fold over the sides of the towel. Serve hot, either completely dry or topped with a small amount of ghee or butter.

Paratha

These breads, called parathas, are flaky and somewhat more elaborate than chapattis or rotis. The dough is rolled out and brushed with ghee or oil folded and brushed with ghee or oil again and folded again to form a layered slice. This is then rolled out again. This is then put on a hot griddle and brushed with oil. The heat makes the layers of dough swell and puff, resulting flaky, pastry like flat breads. They may also be used as snacks, lunch-box favourites, light brunch items or travelling munching companions. Allow 1 or 2 per person.

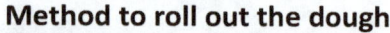

Ingredients:
2.5 cups chapatti flour
1 cup water at room temperature
1 cup chapatti flour
ghee for brushing the bread

Method to roll out the dough
Prepare Basic dough and allow to rest for 1 1/2 to 2 hours. To make triangular-shaped parathas, divide the dough into peach-size balls. With a rolling pin, roll out 1 ball to a circle 5 inches in diameter. Brush the circle of dough with ghee, and fold in half to from a crescent then brush again with ghee and fold into a triangle. Seal the edges well. Dust the paratha with finely sieved whole wheat flour and roll into a large, flat triangle or round paratha. Try to make the edges slightly thinner to ensure uniform cooking. Rather than shaping all the parathas at one time, cook each one as the next one is rolled out.

Method of cooking the paratha
Preheat a cast-iron tawa over medium heat. Place the rolled dough on the palm of one hand and flip it over on to the tawa. When the colour changes on the top and bubbles appear, brush ghee over the surface of the paratha and turn it over. Repeat the process of brushing the paratha on the other side. Keep flipping it over till both sides are browned and spots appear on the paratha. With experience the paratha will puff on the tawa.
To keep the parathas warm as they are cooked, place them in a towel-lined bowl and fold over the sides of the towel. Serve hot.

Poori

These are small round pancakes size rounds of dough that are slipped into hot oil or ghee, where they fill with steam and balloon in seconds. Pooris are soft silk like breads with which curries and vegetables are scooped up.   Allow 2-3 per person, depending on the size of the breads and the accompanying dishes.

Ingredients:
2.5 cups chapatti flour
2/3 cup water at room temperature
ghee
Oil for deep frying

Method to roll out the dough
Make stiff but pliable dough.
Cover the dough with damp cloth
And set aside for 30 minutes.
Knead dough a little again. Dough should be stiff enough to roll without extra flour.
Make small balls of the dough and cover them with damp cloth.
Take one ball of dough and dip a corner of ball in melted ghee or oil and roll it out into 4 to 5 inches round.
Repeat the same process to roll out all pooris.

Frying the Pooris
Heat plenty of oil in a kadhai until very hot.
Put in a poori and immediately start flickering hot oil over the top of it with a spatula so that it will swell up like a ball.
This should take only a few seconds. Flip the poori over and cook the other side until golden brown.
Serve hot with curries or vegetables.

Potato Paratha

Parathas are sometimes stuffed with herbed potatoes, shredded radishes and cauliflower with its water squeezed out, peas and even sugar or dried fruit pastes. Cut into wedges, they are excellent finger foods for parties. Allow 1-2 per person, depending on the size of the breads and the accompanying dishes. Serve with yogurt raita and Indian pickles.

Ingredients:
2 medium potatoes (boiled, peeled, mashed and cooled to room temperature)
1 tsp. Coriander powder
1 tsp. Cumin powder
1/2 tsp. amchoor powder/mango powder
1 green chilli minced (optional)
1 tsp. Chilli powder
1 tsp. lime/lemon juice
salt to taste
finely chopped cilantro
2 cups wheat flour ,

Method:
Mix mashed potatoes, coriander powder, cumin powder, mango powder, chopped green chillies, salt, cilantro, lime juice and chilli powder.
Make small balls of the mixture.
Take a ball of dough slightly thicker than chapatti (large egg size or peach size) and roll it to a circle 4-5 inches in diameter.
Place Potato mixture on it and again make it into a ball.
Seal the edges completely so that the stuffing does not come out.
Flatten these balls and roll into a 6 inch circle.
Pre-heat the griddle (tawa). Turn it and spread little oil or butter and cook over low heat.
Turn it again and spread butter/oil on the other side.
Cook both sides till golden brown.
Serve with chutney, yogurt, steamed vegetable and Indian pickles

---

Bhakari

2 cups whole wheat flour
1 teaspoon salt
2 tablespoons vegetable oil
1/4 cup milk
1/2 cup water

Bhakari Recipe Directions:
Combine the flour, salt, oil, milk, and half the water in a bowl. Mix using a wooden spoon or fingers. Add more water, 1 tablespoon (15 ml) at a time until the dough forms a ball. Knead the dough with lightly oiled hands for 10 minutes. The dough should be fairly firm. Allow the dough to rest, covered with a dish cloth, for 15 minutes.

Divide the dough into 4 to 6 pieces. Roll each piece into a round 1/4 inch thick. Heat a flat griddle or large skillet over moderate heat. Cook the dough, one piece at a time, pressing it down occasionally with a spatula, until cooked and lightly browned on the bottom. Turn the dough and repeat. The dough may balloon slightly during cooking. Repeat with remaining pieces of dough. Makes 4 to 6 pieces.

Fried Bread Puffs

1 cup whole wheat flour
1/2 cup all-purpose flour
1/4 teaspoon salt
2 tablespoons vegetable oil

Directions for Fried Bread Puffs Recipe:
Combine flours, salt and oil in a bowl and make a stiff dough by adding water. Knead dough for 10 to 12 minutes. Wrap in plastic wrap and set aside for 20 minutes.

Break off small pieces of dough about the size of a cherry tomato. Roll out to about 3 inches in diameter. Deep fry in vegetable oil over medium heat a few seconds. They should puff up. Drain on paper towelling and serve hot.

Naan

4 cups all-purpose flour
1 Tablespoon sugar
1 Tablespoon double acting baking powder
1/4 teaspoon baking soda
1/2 tsp salt
2 eggs
1 cup milk
4 to 6 teaspoons ghee or melted butter

Directions for Naan Recipe:
Combine the dry ingredients in a large mixing bowl and stir until the ingredients are thoroughly mixed. Make a well in the centre of the mixture and add the eggs, stirring them into the mixture. Add the milk in a thin stream (or a little at a time if you only have two hands), and stir until all the ingredients are well combined.

Gather the dough into a ball and knead for about 10 minutes, adding a little flour as needed to prevent sticking, until the dough is smooth and can be gathered into a soft, somewhat sticky ball. Moisten your hands with a teaspoon of ghee, rub it over the ball of dough,
and place it in a bowl. Drape a kitchen towel over the bowl and allow to sit at room temperature for about 3 hours.

Place two increased baking sheets in the oven and preheat the oven and the sheets to 450F. Divide the dough into 6 equal pieces and flatten each into a tear drop, or leaf shape about 6 inches long and 31/2 inches across at its widest point. Use your fingers to do this, and moisten them with ghee as needed to prevent the dough from sticking. The ghee also assures the proper texture of the bread, so moisten your fingers with it even if the dough is not sticky.

Arrange the bread leaves side by side on the preheated baking sheets and bake them for about 6 minutes, or until they are firm to the touch. Slide them under the broiler for a minute or so to brown the tops lightly. Serve warm or at room temperature.

You can add almost anything to a Naan bread whilst in the preparation stage like garlic, cooked minced meats, cooked potato, coconut, cooked chicken etc.

APPETISERS

Aloo Bonda

Ingredients:
2 or 3 medium potatoes (boiled and peeled and loosely mashed)
1/2 tsp. of cumin and mustard seeds each
fresh green chilli chopped finely - to taste
1/2 tsp. each ginger & garlic(finely chopped)
3/4th cup Chopped Onions
1/4 tsp. turmeric powder
1/2 cup. Cilantro leaves (chopped)
Salt to taste
2 tbsp. Lemon juice
1 1/2 cups besan -chickpea flour
1 tsp. Cayenne Pepper
1/4 tsp. baking Soda
Oil for deep frying - use a wok for frying

Method:
1. Heat about two tablespoons of oil. Add mustard seeds and when the seeds start to crackle, add the cumin seeds, green chilli, salt, ginger and garlic. Fry for a few seconds and add onions and turmeric powder. When the onions start to turn brown add cilantro and lemon juice and the potatoes. Mix well and turn off the heat. Let this mixture cool. Shape into small balls.
2. Make a thick batter with Besan/Chickpea flour, salt, red chilli powder, baking soda and water.
3. Heat the oil for 10 to 15 minutes on medium heat. When the oil is hot, Dip the potato balls into the batter and carefully drop in the oil. Turn it every four minutes and remove from oil when it turns golden brown.
4. Serve with tamarind or green chutney.

Pakoda,

Ingredients:
1 1/2 cups besan (gram flour)
1/2 tsp. red chilli powder (cayenne pepper)
Salt to taste
1 cup potatoes or onions (sliced)
4 tbsp. minced cilantro
1/4 cup fresh fenugreek/methi leaves or 2 tbsp. dried (optional)
Oil for deep frying

Method:
1. Mix the onions, cayenne pepper, salt and besan (also cilantro and methi). Let it rest for about 10 minutes to allow the vegetables to sweat. Add some water (only as much as required) to make into a very thick paste.
2. Heat the oil for about 10 to 15 minutes on medium heat. Pour a spoonful of the paste in the oil and let fry until golden brown. Stir in between. Remove from oil and strain the oil out.
3. Serve with tamarind chutney and mint chutney

Samosa

For the pastry:
   2 cups flour
   1/2 tsp. salt
   4 Tbsp. oil
   4 Tbsp. water

For the stuffing:
   4-5 medium potatoes, boiled in their jackets and allowed to cool
   4 Tbsp. oil
   1 medium onion, peeled and finely chopped
   1 cup (175 g) shelled peas
   1 Tbsp. finely grated peeled fresh ginger
   1 fresh hot green chilli, finely chopped
   3 Tbsp. very finely chopped fresh green coriander (cilantro)
   3 Tbsp. water
   1 1/2 tsp. salt
   1 tsp. ground coriander seeds
   1 tsp. Garam Masala

1 tsp. ground roasted cumin seeds
1/4 tsp. cayenne pepper
2 Tbsp. lemon juice
oil for deep frying

Sift the flour and salt into a bowl. Add the 4 tablespoons on oil and rub it in with your fingers until the mixture resembles coarse breadcrumbs. Slowly add about 4 tablespoons water -- or a tiny bit more -- and gather the dough into a stiff ball.

Empty the ball out on to clean work surface. Knead the dough for about 10 minutes or until it is smooth. Make a ball. Rub the ball with about 1/4 teaspoon oil and slip it into a plastic bag. Set aside for 30 minutes or longer.

Make the stuffing. Peel the potatoes and cut them into 1/4 inch dice. Heat 4 tablespoons oil in a large frying pan over a medium flame. When hot, put in the onion. Stir and fry until brown at the edges. Add the peas, ginger, green chilli, fresh coriander (cilantro), and 3 tablespoons water. Cover, lower heat and simmer until peas are cooked. Stir every now and then and add a little more water if the frying pan seems to dry out.

Add the diced potatoes, salt, coriander seeds, Garam Masala, roasted cumin, cayenne, and lemon juice. Stir to mix. Cook on low heat for 3-4 minutes, stirring gently as you do so. Check balance of salt and lemon juice. You may want more of both. Turn off the heat and allow the mixture to cool.

Knead the pastry dough again and divide it into eight balls. Keep 7 covered while you work with the eight. Roll this ball out into a 7 inch (18 cm) round. Cut it into half with a sharp, pointed knife. Pick up one half and form a cone, making a 1/4 inch wide (5 mm), and overlapping seam. Glue this seam together with a little water. Fill the cone with about 2 1/2 tablespoons of the potato mixture. Close the top of the cone by sticking the open edges together with a little water. Again, your seam should be about 1/4 inch (5 mm) wide. Press the top seam down with the prongs of a fork or flute it with your fingers. Make 7 more samosas.

Heat about 1 1/2 to 2 inches (4-5 cm) of oil for deep frying over a medium-low flame. You may use a small, deep, frying pan for this or an Indian wok. When the oil is medium hot, put in as many samosas as the pan will hold in a single layer. Fry slowly, turning the samosas frequently until they are golden brown and crisp. Drain on paper towel and serve hot, warm, or at room temperature.

Aloo Tikki,

Ingredients:
6 oiled and peeled potatoes mashed
fresh green chilli chopped finely - to taste
1 tsp. ginger (finely chopped)
1/2 cup. Cilantro leaves (chopped)
1 tsp. cayenne pepper
1 tbsp. coriander powder
Salt to taste
1 tsp. cumin powder
1 tsp. mango powder called amchur
Oil for pan frying

Method:
1. Boil the potato. Cool. Peel the skin and mash the potato.
2. Mix all ingredients except the oil.
3. Make small hamburger size patties but about 1/2 inch high.
4. Pan Fry in a non-stick pan with oil until both sides are golden brown.
5. Serve with tamarind or green chutney.

Bhel Puri

2 cups puffed rice
1 cup cooked chickpeas
2 medium potatoes, cooked, peeled and cubed
1 small onion, finely chopped
2 oz. crushed potato chips
2 oz. salted peanuts
1 tbsp. tomato sauce
1/2 tsp. salt or to taste

Directions:
Mix the puffed rice, chickpeas, potatoes, onions and peanuts. Add tomato sauce, mix well and then sprinkle salt and the sev/potato chips. The mixture must be made immediately before serving, or the puffed rice will turn soggy

Bhindi Dopeaza

1 lb. okra
2 medium onions, chopped
1/4 teaspoon garlic paste or powder
1/4 teaspoon coriander paste or powder
1/8 teaspoon cumin
3 large tomatoes
2 tablespoon oil
1/2 cup chopped cilantro

Directions:
Cut the tip and the very bottom from the okra just to clean it, but do not slice. Heat oil in a pan over medium heat. Add onion and cook for 3 minutes. Add all ingredients except okra, tomato and cilantro. Cook for 3 minutes. Add okra, and then cook for 6 to 8 minutes. Garnish with tomato and cilantro. Serve with rice, Naan or pita bread.

Cheela Tomato

1 pound tomatoes, peeled and pureed
1 pound besan or gram flour
4 green chillies, minced
1 small bunch of coriander leaves, minced
1 teaspoon til (sesame seeds)
1 teaspoon turmeric powder
Salt and chilli powder to taste
6 teaspoons sugar

Recipe Directions:
1. Form a soft batter by mixing together all the above ingredients.
2. Heat a griddle (tawa) to smoking. Then lower the heat and grease it well with ghee.
3. Put 1/4 cup of batter on it and spread it into a thin even round shape. When the undersides turn golden, put a little more ghee around the edges and turn over.
4. Remove from heat when both sides turn golden brown. Serve piping hot with green chutney

Masala Parathas

1 cup wheat flour
1/2 cup rice or all purpose flour
1 onion
1 carrot
3 to 4 cabbage leaves
Cayenne Pepper to taste
1 jalapeno or Serrano pepper
1 potato
4 green chillies
1/2 teaspoon grated fresh ginger
5 tablespoons vegetable oil
1/4 teaspoon turmeric powder
Salt to taste

Directions:
Finely chop all the vegetables either in a chopper or by hand in a large plate. You may even grate them if a chopper is not available. Add the flours, 2 tablespoons oil, salt, cayenne, turmeric and knead to very stiff dough. Do not keep the dough for long after kneading, or it will become gooey and soft. This would make it difficult to roll the parathas.

Divide into 3 parts. Roll into 5.inch rounds. Shallow fry on a hot griddle (tawa) on both sides until golden brown using the remaining oil. Eat hot or carry away for later, with sauce, tamarind or onion chutney.

Masoor Dhal & Onions

2/3 cup masoor dhal
1 tbsp. oil
1 large onion, sliced
1 tsp. turmeric powder
2 tsp. salt or to taste

Recipe Directions:
Pre cook the lentils using three cups of water. Heat oil in a saucepan and fry the onions for five minutes, stirring constantly. Add the lentils and another three cups of water and turmeric powder, heat till the mixture starts boiling, season with salt and turn off the heat.

Paneer Cheese

12 cups whole milk
2 teaspoon salt
1/4 teaspoon cumin seed, crushed
1/3 cup lemon juice

Directions:
In a 5 quart Dutch oven bring milk, salt and cumin seed just to boiling; reduce heat. Simmer, uncovered, for 5 minutes. Remove from heat. Stir in lemon juice. Let stand 15 minutes.

Line a large strainer or colander with several layers of pure cotton cheesecloth. Strain mixture; discard liquid. Gently squeeze the cheesecloth to remove as much liquid from the curds as possible. Wrap cloth around curds. Place wrapped curds in a large strainer or colander and put a weighted bowl on top to help press out any additional liquid. Let stand, covered, in the refrigerator for at least 15 hours.

Remove curds. Discard liquid. Form curds into a flat rectangle or press into a large bowl to shape. Refrigerate, covered with plastic wrap, until well chilled. Store in refrigerator, tightly wrapped, for up to 3 weeks. Yields about 1 pound.

SOUPS

There are mainly 2 types of soup in India the south Indian Rasam and the North Indian Shorba.
Rasam normally forms the second course in a traditional South Indian menu. There are various ways of preparing it. It is normally mixed with plain cooked rice and eaten with different curries for side dish. It makes for a very good appetizer or soup also when taken all by itself. Serve as a soup with papa dams or with steamed rice.
Shorba is the Indian name for soup and is a North Indian dish.

Tomato Appetizer soup -Tomato Rasam - Kerala

Ingredients:
Serves: 4
8 oz. or 250 gm tomatoes, diced
1 onion, chopped
4 cloves garlic, crushed

4 green chillies, chopped
1 tsp. tamarind pulp
1 tbsp. jaggery
1 tsp. mustard seeds
10 curry leaves (optional)
1 red chilli, broken into two
1 tsp. coriander seeds – roasted & powdered
1 tsp. cumin seeds + 2 tsp. peppercorns – roasted & powdered
½ tbsp. oil

Method:
1. Boil the tomatoes, chillies and garlic in 4 cups of water.
2. Add the ground spices, jaggery and tamarind pulp and simmer for 15 minutes.
3. Heat the oil. Add mustard seeds until they splutter. Add the curry leaves, red chilli, asafoetida powder and onion and fry for a minute.
4. Pour it over the tomatoes. Heat and serve the rasam garnished with chopped cilantro/coriander leaves

Lemon Pepper Rasam - South India

Ingredients:
Serves: 4
1/4 cup toor dal
1 cup water
a piece of fresh ginger (2 1/2 cm, 1 in), peeled and grated
4 green chills
1/2 tsp. cumin seeds
3/4 tsp. black peppercorns
1 1/2 cups water
1/2 tsp. ground turmeric
salt to taste
2 tomatoes, quartered
juice of 1 lemon
coriander leaves, chopped to garish
For Seasoning:
2 tsp. ghee
1 tsp. brown mustard seeds
1/2 tsp. asafoetida powder
1 red Chile, halved
a few curry leaves

Method:
Wash Toro dal well. Drain. Place dal in a heavy saucepan. Cover with 1 cup water

and bring to the boil. When boiling, cover pan with a lid, leaving slightly ajar. Lower the heat, and simmer dal gently for 45 minutes to 1 hour or until soft. Stir several times during the last 30 minutes of cooking. (The water should be mostly gone). Set dal aside without draining.

Using an electric blender or food processor, blend the fresh ginger and green chills into a paste. Now blend or process the cumin seeds and black peppercorns into a powder. Set both aside.

Place the un-drained cooked dal in a heavy saucepan. Add 1 1/2 cups extra water, ground turmeric, salt to taste, and ginger/chilli paste. Slowly bring to the boil.

Seasoning:

Heat 2 tsp. ghee in a heavy frying pan or skillet. Add mustard seeds, asafoetida powder, halved red chilli, a few curry leaves, and pepper/cumin seed powder. When the mustard seeds splutter, add this mixture to the rasam. Turn off the heat and add the lemon juice.

Garnish with cilantro/coriander leaves. Serve hot with rice.

Dal Shorba   (Punjab)

Ingredients:
Serves: 4-5
1 cup masoor dal
3 onions, sliced
4 cloves crushed garlic
1/2 teaspoon chilli powder (optional)
3 teaspoons curry powder
3 tomatoes, cut into big pieces
6 tablespoons chopped spinach leaves
1 tablespoon oil
salt and lime juice to taste

Method:
Heat the oil in a pot and fry the onions for a few seconds.
Add the crushed garlic, chilli and curry powders. Fry again for a few seconds.
Add 6 teacups of water, the tomatoes and washed masoor dal and cook in a pressure cooker.
When cooked, blend in a blender.
Boil for 15 minutes. Add salt.
Just before serving, add the spinach and boil for a few seconds. Serve hot with a slice of lemon.

Gobhi Shorba (Cauliflower Soup)

Ingredients:
Serves: 4-6
1 Quart/litre milk
10 cashews finely chopped
1 tsp. butter
2 cups water
8 oz/1/4 kg cauliflower flowerets cut into cubes
1 tsp. sugar
salt to taste
freshly ground pepper to taste
a pinch of roasted and ground cumin as the garnish

Method:
1. Heat cauliflower, cashews, water and milk over low flame for 15-20 min. Let it cool.
2. Blend the mixture.
3. Add salt, sugar and pepper.
4. Boil the mixture. Stir in the butter near boiling point.
5. Serve immediately garnished with coriander leaves and roasted cumin.

Lamb Shorba

Ingredients:
1 medium onion, chopped
1 large clove garlic, chopped
dried red pepper flakes to taste.
3/4 pound lamb or goat shoulder, Trimmed of as much fat as possible and cut into small (1/2-inch) cubes
2 fresh tomatoes, skinned, seeded and roughly chopped
1 can 12 oz. garbanzo
2 cups water or more if you like
1/2 cup yogurt
Spices
1 teaspoon cumin
1/2 teaspoon dry mint
1/2 teaspoon cinnamon
1 cardamom
1/2 teaspoon salt
few sprigs saffron

Method:
Heat the oil in a pot and fry the onions for a few seconds.
Add the crushed garlic, chilli flakes and lamb. Fry again for a few seconds. Add

spices and sauté for few more moments.
Add all ingredients except the yogurt. Simmer till the lamb is very well done and has absorbed all the flavours.
Before serving bring the heat to low add yogurt and serve hot.

SALADS

Indian salads are simple salads usually consisting of cucumbers, tomatoes, radish, red onions, carrots sprinkled with salt and roasted crushed cumin or sautéed mustard seeds. They may have fresh coconut, peanuts and fried dal added to them for flavouring. They are then sprinkled with lime or lemon juice. Salads in India are not served separately during a meal. They are like a fresh condiment along with the meal. When they are served separately they are like a fresh snack. Indian salads are meant to take advantage of seasonal produce and in hot summer these vegetables with their cool water content, and lime juice make for a cooling treat.

Salad South Indian Style

Ingredients:
1 carrot, peeled and julienne
1 cucumber, peeled and diced
1 tomato, diced
1 green chilli (chilli pepper), minced
1 small bunch of cilantro, coriander leaves minced
salt and pepper to taste
2 tablespoons lemon/lime juice
For Salad Dressing
2 teaspoons oil
1 teaspoon brown mustard seeds
1 teaspoon black gram dal (washed urad dal), picked over and rinsed
1 red chilli (chilli pepper), halved
1/2 teaspoon asafoetida powder
a few curry leaves (optional)

Method:
Add the first 7 ingredients in a bowl and mix thoroughly. Set aside.
Making the salad dressing: Heat 2 teaspoons oil in a heavy pan or skillet. Add the mustard seeds, black gram dal, halved red chilli, asafoetida, and a few curry leaves. When the mustard seeds splutter, add this mixture to the vegetables. Now add the lemon juice, and mix thoroughly. Serve at room temperature.

Salad North Indian Style

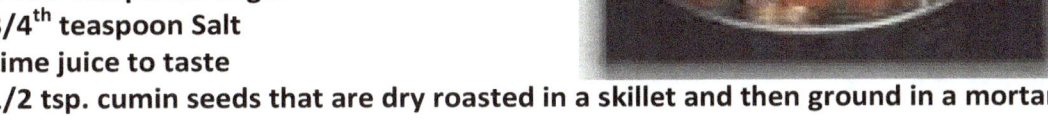

Ingredients:
2 to 3 large Tomatoes, diced
2 large Cucumber, peeled and finely diced
1/4th cup Onion, finely diced
1 Green chilli, finely chopped
A few sprigs of Coriander / Cilantro leaves
1 to 2 teaspoons Sugar
3/4th teaspoon Salt
Lime juice to taste
1/2 tsp. cumin seeds that are dry roasted in a skillet and then ground in a mortar

Method:
Add all the ingredients in a bowl and mix thoroughly. Set aside.
Serve at room temperature.

Chaat (Fiery Fruit Salad) North Indian Style

In Indian, this nuclear fusion fruit salad is sold from sidewalk stands as a cooling snack on hot days. Serve with milder main dishes to assure survival to dessert.

Ingredients:
3 lbs. of mixed fruit in season peeled,
De-seeded and cut in 1 cm. cubes
Banana and oranges are a must.
Apple, pear, nectarine, plums, guava, mango,
Pitted cherries, pineapple, kiwi, seedless grapes.
4 tbsp. fresh lemon juice
2 tsp. cayenne
1 tsp. cumin seeds, roasted and crushed into a powder
1 tsp. paprika
1 tsp. salt
1 tsp. black pepper
1/2 tsp. mint
1 tsp. powdered ginger (optional)

Place all fruit in a large serving bowl and mix in lemon juice. Mix all the spices in a separate bowl, pour over the fruit and mix well with your hands. Cover the bowl with plastic wrap and refrigerate until well chilled, at least 1 hour. Makes 6 servings

Aunas Ambo Sasam (Mango/Pineapple Fruit Salad) Southwest Indian Style

Ingredients - serves 4
4 cups mixed fruits chopped (pineapple, mango, apple and green or black grapes depending on availability)
4 tablespoons fresh grated coconut
2 dry red chillies
1 teaspoon(s) mustard seeds
2 tablespoon(s) sugar or as per taste
salt to taste

Method:
Mix the sugar into the chopped fruits and keep aside.
Grind the coconut with the red chillies and a little water. When almost done, add the mustard seeds. Grind for a few more seconds till the mustard seeds are crushed. Add the coconut paste to the fruits with salt and mix well.
Serve cold or at room temperature.

Sprouted Moong dal Salad South Indian Style

Ingredients
2 cups sprouted green gram or moong dal
4 tbsp. onions finely chopped
2 cups tomato and cucumber chopped
2 big lettuce leaves sliced fine
2 tbsp. roasted peanuts
a dash of lemon and salt to taste

Method:
1. gently mix all the ingredients except the roasted peanuts in a salad bowl. Keep refrigerated.
2. Mix in the roasted peanuts just before serving.
3. Serve cold.

Salad Gujarati or West Indian Style Salad

Ingredients:
5 carrots, trimmed, peeled, and coarsely grated
1/4 tsp. salt
2 tbsp. vegetable oil
1 tbsp. whole black mustard seeds
2 tsp. lemon juice
1 tablespoon fresh grated coconut or coconut flakes

Method

Toss grated carrots with salt. Heat oil over medium flame until very hot, add mustard seeds. When they begin to pop, pour contents of pan-oil and seeds-over carrots. Add lemon juice and toss. Add the grated coconut. Mix thoroughly. Serve at room temperature

KEBABS

Saffron and Cream Sauce (North India)

A popular Kebab sauce used in North India

Ingredients:
Serves: 6
1/8 teaspoon saffron strands
2 tablespoons boiling water
2 tablespoons blanched pistachios
4 tablespoons blanched almonds
1 tablespoon ghee or butter
3/4 cup cream
1/2 cup milk
1/2 teaspoon ground cardamom
1/2 teaspoon salt or to taste
1/2 teaspoon white pepper.

Method:
Pound saffron in mortar and pestle, then dissolve in the boiling water. Put pistachios and almonds into electric blender and grind finely, or pound with mortar and pestle. Heat the ghee or butter in a small pan and fry the ground nuts, stirring constantly. Add the saffron, cream, milk, cardamom, salt and pepper and simmer, stirring constantly, until sauce is thick. Serve with kebabs.

Skewered Barbecued Lamb - Hussaini Kebab

Ingredients: Serves 6
2 kg (4 lb) leg of lamb, boned
1 teaspoon crushed garlic
11/2 teaspoons finely grated fresh ginger
1 teaspoon freshly ground black pepper
2 tablespoons finely ground almonds
2 tablespoons yoghurt
1 teaspoon ground coriander
1 teaspoon ground cumin
Salt to taste
2 tablespoons sesame oil
1 tablespoon lemon juice

Method:
Trim lamb, discarding excess fat. Any sinewy bits may be saved for stock or for adding to a curry. Cut the lean meat into 2.5 cm (1 inch) cubes and put into a large bowl.

Combine all the remaining ingredients, mixing well. Marinate lamb in the mixture, kneading the spices well into the meat. Cover and leave for 2 or 3 hours, or refrigerate and leave for as long as 4 days.

Thread 4 or 5 pieces of meat on each skewer and barbecue over glowing coals or under a preheated griller until crisp and brown all over, turning to ensure lamb is well cooked. Serve with parathas and Indian sas (sauce) which is given above.

Minced Meat on Skewers (North India) - Seekh Kebab

Ingredients: Serves
750 g (1 1/2 lb)
1 teaspoon crushed garlic
f teaspoon finely grated fresh ginger
2 teaspoons salt
1 1/2 teaspoons Garam Masala
2 tablespoons roasted chick peas, ground, or besan (chick pea flour)
2 tablespoons ground almonds
2 tablespoons finely chopped fresh coriander
I fresh green chilli, seeded and finely chopped
2 tablespoons yoghurt
1 tablespoon lemon juice

Method:
1. Combine all the ingredients and mix thoroughly, kneading well until mixture becomes very smooth. Divide between 6 skewers and shape into long sausages. (Use skewers that are rectangular in cross-section, because the -mixture will slip on round skewers.) Cook over glowing coals on a barbecue or under a preheated griller until browned on all sides and cooked through. Serve with rice or Indian bread, or as part of a waswan feast

Minced Lamb and Lentil Patties (Uttar Pradesh) Shami Kebab

Makes 8 large or 24 cocktail size patties

Ingredients:
750 g (1 1/2 lb) finely minced lamb
1 medium onion, finely chopped
3 tablespoons yellow split peas (mattar dhal) or red lentils (masoor dhal) _
1 teaspoon finely grated fresh ginger
$1^1/2$ teaspoons finely chopped garlic
salt to taste
2 cups water
1/2 teaspoon Garam Masala
1 tablespoon yoghurt or thick cream
1 small egg, beaten
ghee or oil for shallow frying

Filling:
1 fresh green chilli, seeded and finely chopped
1 tablespoon finely chopped fresh cilantro
I spring onion, including green leaves
1/2 teaspoon finely grated fresh ginger

Method:
Put lamb, onion, dhal, ginger, garlic, salt and water into a heavy saucepan and bring to the boll stirring. Cover and heat over low heat until meat, lentils and onions are soft, about 45 minutes. Then uncover and cook, stirring now and then, until all the liquid has been absorbed. This may take at least 1 hour. Leave to cool, and then mix in the Garam Masala and yoghurt or cream. Add I tablespoon of beaten egg and mix well. If mixture is not too moist add more of the beaten egg. Knead very well for 10 minutes or until mixture is completely smooth.

Divide into 8 portions and form each into a flat circle. Put 14 teaspoonful of filling in the middle. Close the meat mixture around it, pinching edges together. Flatten gently to form a small round patty. Shallow fry on a heavy griddle or frying pan light greased with ghee or oil. Serve hot. If serving these as cocktail snacks and making them bite-size, it is easier not to use a filling but to serve with mint chutney from our Chutney section for dipping.

SNACKS

Instant Rice Pilaf - Kaande Pohe

Ingredients:
2 cup Pohe (Flaked, beaten rice),
1 small onion,
1 potato,
3-4 green chillies,
1 teaspoon lemon juice,
2-3 teaspoon sugar,
salt to taste,
1 tbspoon oil,
2 teaspoon mustard seeds,
1 teaspoon asafoetida,
2 teaspoon turmeric powder,
coconut and coriander leaves for garnishing.

Method:
1. Soak Pohe in water. Drain water and keep it aside for 10 to 15 minutes.
2. Now rub some salt, sugar and lemon juice to it.
3. Chop green chillies, onion and potatoes.
4. Heat oil in a pan. Add mustard seeds. When they splutter, add asafoetida, turmeric powder, onion pieces, potato pieces and green chillies.
5. When potatoes turn tender, add pohe and stir.
6. Cover and cook for sometime. Remove the lid, stir and again allow it to cook for 2 minutes.
7. Garnish with coconut and coriander leaves. Serve hot.

Tapioca Pilaf - Sabudana khichdi

Ingredients:
2 cup sago or Tapioca
1 potato diced small
3-4 green chillies,
1 teaspoon lemon juice (optional),
1 small piece ginger (optional),
1/2 cup peanut bits
2-3 teaspoon sugar,
salt to taste,
1 tbspoon oil,
2 teaspoon cumin seeds,
coconut and coriander leaves for garnishing.

Method:
1. Soak sago/tapioca in water. Drain the water and keep it aside for half an hour to one hour.
2. Now add peanut powder, salt, sugar and lemon juice and mix the tapioca
3. Cut green chillies into small pieces and grate ginger.
4. Heat oil or ghee in a pan.
6. Add cumin seeds, potato pieces and chillies.
7. As soon as potatoes are tender, add sago and stir. Continue to cook tapioca by carefully turning the tapioca as to cook all of it.
8. Garnish with coconut and coriander leaves. Serve hot.

Semolina Pilaf – Upma

Ingredients:
1 cup semolina
2 cups water
3-4 cashews broken
1 teaspoon Urad dal (optional)
1\4 teaspoon mustard seeds
1 tablespoon oil
2 green chillies diced
Small piece of ginger chopped thin
Half a dozen curry leaves (optional)
3\4 teaspoon salt
1 cup vegetables like carrots, peas, cauliflower beans in bite size and slightly steamed in the microwave or pan
1 chopped onion
1 tablespoon of salt free butter or Ghee
Lime juice, salt to taste

Method:
1. Heat the oil in a sauce pan. Add chena dal, urad dal, mustard seeds and heat on a low fire. When the dal's become light brown and the mustard seeds crack up, add the green chillies, ginger, onion and curry leaves.
2. when the onions are cooked soft, add peas and carrots. Sauté for 1 minute
3. Add 2 cups of water and salt. When water starts boiling add one cup of cream of wheat continuously stirring. Then add one table spoon of butter.
3. Reduce the heat and cook till it becomes a soft pudding. Remove from fire and keep it for 5 minutes. Add lime juice and salt to taste
4. Serve with tomato/ginger chutney or any other chutney or pickle.

Semolina Pilaf Bombay style - Khara Rava Bombay Style

Ingredients:
1 cup(s) semolina (or cream of wheat)
1 medium onion(s) sliced finely
4 tablespoons ghee (clarified butter) / butter
1 teaspoon(s) each of mustard and cumin seeds
1 teaspoon(s) ginger chopped
2 green chillies slit / chopped
2 tablespoon(s) grated coconut if available
4 curry leaves
2 cup(s) water
salt to taste

Fry cashew nuts and finely chopped coriander leaves to garnish
Heat half of the ghee (clarified butter) in a pan. Fry semolina, stirring continuously, to a golden colour on medium / low level for about 2 minute(s). Keep aside.

Heat the remaining ghee (clarified butter) in a pan. Toss in the mustard seeds followed by the cumin seeds and fry till the seeds splutter fully. Add the onion(s), ginger, green chillies and stir fry on medium level for about 3 minutes or till the onions are transparent and soft.

Mix in the semolina, curry leaves and salt. Add water to this and mix well. Cover and cook on low heat for about 3 minutes or till the mixture is almost dry. Garnish with fried cashew nuts, grated coconut and finely chopped coriander leaves

---

Parsi Poro Pan Omelette (Parsi)

Ingredients:
Serves: 2
1 cup diced potato
2 tablespoons ghee or oil 4 eggs
Salt to taste
1/4 teaspoon black pepper
1/2 teaspoon ground cumin
2 tablespoons finely chopped fresh cilantro/coriander leaves
1 small onion, finely chopped
2 fresh red or green chillies, seeded and chopped

Method:
Parboil potato in lightly salted boiling water for a minute or two, drain well in colander.
Heat ghee or oil in a frying pan and fry the potato until lightly browned. Lift out on slotted spoon and set aside. Separate eggs and beat the whites until frothy, then beat in the yolks, salt, pepper and cumin. Fold in coriander, onion and chillies. Golden brown on bottom, turn omelette over and cook until brown on other side. Serve hot with chapattis or bread.

Akoori - Scrambled Eggs (Parsi)

Ingredients:
Serves: 4-6
6-8 eggs
4 tablespoons milk
Salt to taste
1/4 teaspoon ground black pepper
2 tablespoons ghee or butter
6 spring onions or
2 small white onions, finely chopped
2-3 fresh red or green chillies, seeded and chopped
1 teaspoon finely grated fresh ginger
1/8 teaspoon ground turmeric
2 tablespoons chopped fresh coriander leaves
1 ripe tomato, peeled and diced, optional
1/2 teaspoon ground cumin
Garnish: tomato wedges
sprig of fresh cilantro/coriander leaves

Method:
Beat eggs until well mixed. Add the milk, salt and pepper. Heat ghee or butter in a large, heavy frying pan and cook the onions, chillies and ginger until soft. Add turmeric, coriander leaves and tomato, if used, and fry for a minute or two longer, and then stir in the egg mixture and the ground cumin. Cook over low heat, stirring and lifting the eggs as they begin to set on the base of the pan. Mix and cook until the eggs are of a creamy consistency-they should not be cooked until dry. Turn on to a serving plate and garnish with tomato and coriander. Serve with chapattis, parathas or toasted bread.

Ekoori

3 tablespoons butter or vegetable oil
1 small onion, finely chopped
1/2 teaspoon peeled and finely grated ginger
1 fresh hot green chilli, finely chopped
1 tablespoon finely chopped coriander
1/8 teaspoon ground turmeric
1/2 teaspoon ground cumin
1 small tomato, peeled and chopped
6 large eggs, lightly beaten
Salt and pepper to taste

Directions:
Melt butter in a medium size non-stick frying pan over a medium heat. Add the onion and sauté until soft. Add ginger, chilli, fresh coriander, turmeric, cumin and tomato. Stir and cook for 3 to 4 minutes until tomatoes are soft.

Put in the beaten eggs and season lightly. Stir the eggs gently until they form thick curds. Cook the scrambled eggs to desired consistency. Serve with toast or Indian bread.

MEAT DISHES
LAMB, BEEF, CHICKEN, PORK.

As suggested at the beginning of this recipe book you can swap individual meats around in any of these dishes.

HONEY AND GINGER CHICKEN SKEWERS

4, boneless skinless
Chicken breast halves (about 1 pound)
1/3 cup, Honey & Ginger Marinade
1, medium bell peppers
(Such as yellow red or orange) cut into 1-inch pieces
8, wooden skewers
Cooked white rice if desired

Soak wooden skewers in cold water for at least 30 minutes. Rinse chicken; pat dry. Cut chicken breasts lengthwise into 1-inch wide strips. Place chicken in large, plastic food storage bag. Add marinade. Let marinate in refrigerator for 2 hours. Meanwhile in boiling water, blanch peppers for 2 minutes. Thread chicken onto skewers in an S-fashion; leaving 1/4-inch spaces between pieces for even cooking. Add 2 pieces of bell pepper to each skewer. Grill or broil until chicken is cooked through; 5-8 minutes. For extra flavour, brush skewers with additional marinade. If desired, serve with rice.
Servings: 4
Cook Time: 30 minutes

INDIAN PIZZA

1 cup	chopped roasted chicken breast
1/2 cup	Sweet Mango Chutney
1	(12-inch) pre baked pizza crust
1/3 cup	Mild Curry Paste
1/2 cup	shredded mozzarella cheese
1/3 cup	raisins
1/3 cup	coconut
1/3 cup	unsalted peanuts

Preheat oven to 425°F. In medium bowl, stir together chicken and mango chutney. Spread pizza crust with curry paste. Top with chicken mixture. Sprinkle with mozzarella, raisins, coconut, and peanuts. Bake 12 to 15 minutes until golden brown.
Servings: 4
Cook Time: 30 minutes

CHICKEN KORMA

1 tablespoon vegetable oil
1 medium onion chopped
1 pound boneless
Skinless chicken breast diced
1/2 cup broccoli florets
1/2 cup sliced carrots
1 Korma Cooking Sauce (15-ounce) jar
3/4 cups half-and-half
2 medium tomatoes seeded and diced

In large skillet, heat oil over medium-high heat. Add onion and chicken; cook until chicken is cooked through, about 3-4 minutes. Add the vegetables and cook for an additional 3 minutes. Stir in Korma Cooking Sauce and simmer for 15 minutes or until the vegetables are cooked through. Stir in half-and-half and tomatoes. Heat until warmed through.
Servings: 4
Cook Time: 30 minutes

CHICKEN SHAHJAHANE

Ingredients
Chicken   1 kg
Onions   250 gm
Ginger   10 gm
Garlic   10 gm
Tomatoes 200 gm
Coriander ½ bunch
Khas-Khas 20 gm
Cream   100 ml

Salt   to taste
Gr. Chillies 1
Cashew nuts 50 gm
Chilly Pow 5 gm
Dhania Pow 5 gm
Haldi Pow 5 gm
Oil 50 ml

Method :

- Clean, cut chicken and apply salt.
- Grind onion, garlic, ginger, green chills.
- Chop coriander and tomatoes.
- Boil and grind khus-khus to a paste.
- Grind cashew nuts to a paste.
- Heat fat, fry ground Masala and add chilli powder, haldi powder, coriander powder, continue frying.
- Add khas-khas, chopped tomatoes.
- Add chicken pieces and sufficient water to cook.
- When chicken is cooked add cashew nuts and coriander leaves.

MURG KA SOLA

INGREDIENTS

Ingredients	Qty
Chicken	1 kg
Garlic	15 gm
Raw papaya	20 gm
Ginger	5 gm
Salt	To taste
Roasted gram flour	5 gm
Red chilli powder	10 gm
Garam Masala	¼ tsp
Khoya/Mawa	25 gm
Sour curd	60 gm
Almonds	15 gm
Ghee	60 gm
Onions	60 gm

METHOD

- Remove the skin of the chicken and cut it into large piece, wash and dry with cloth.
- Prick the pieces well with the fork. Wrap ground papaya on the pieces and marinate for 4hrs.
- Than wipe off the papaya or wash it mix well all the ingredients except ghee and apply over the chicken piece.
- Take a skewer and put the pieces on the skewer taking care that the Masala remains on the pieces.
- Cook it on the live charcoal or in the over basting occasionally.
- Cook till they are tender. Remove and serve with chutney and onion rings.

MUTTON/LAMB ROGAN JOSH

Ingredients
Mutton   500 gm
Tomatoes 115 gm
Coriander 10 gm
Fat   30 gm
Chilly powder 10 gm
Ginger   10 gm
Garlic   5 gm
Onions   115 gm
Ratan Jot 5 gm
Salt   To taste

Method :

- Cut mutton into small pieces.
- Chop onions, grind it with red chilly ginger and garlic
- Heat fat, fry Masala, add meat pieces fry well and add sufficient water to cook meat.
- Dissolve Ratan Jot in a little warm water and add to meat and look on slow fire.
- Garnish with coriander.

Lamb Braised in Yogurt and Cream

1 cup plain yogurt
1 cup heavy cream
2 medium onions, coarsely chopped
1/4 cup blanched almonds
2 tablespoons chopped fresh ginger
2 tablespoons ground coriander
1 tablespoon ground cardamom
Salt and freshly ground pepper to taste
2 lb. boneless lean lamb, cut into 2-inch pieces
1 to 2 lb. potatoes, peeled and quartered

Combine all ingredients except the lamb and potatoes in an electric blender or food processor and process until smooth. Put the yogurt mixture and the lamb into a large, heavy pot (preferably non-stick) and bring to a boil over moderate heat. Reduce the heat and simmer tightly covered for 2 hours.

Check the stew and stir frequently, adding milk or water as needed if the sauce becomes too thick. Add the potatoes and continue cooking until tender, 30 to 45 minutes.

Chicken Curry from the Indian State of Kerala

Ingredients:
Chicken- 2 Lbs. (wash & cut into pieces)
Fresh green peas or green and red bell pepper- 1/4 cup
Carrot- 1 (cut into thin strips)
Small baby potatoes- 7 boiled and peeled
Onions- 2 (chopped)
Grated ginger- 1.5 inch piece
Garlic- 6 cloves (chopped)
Green chillies- 3
Coconut milk- 1 1/2 cups
- Spices -
Cinnamon- 1 piece
Bay leaves- 2
Cloves- 2
Black peppercorns- 1 tsp.
Turmeric powder- 1/2 tsp.
Garam Masala powder- 1/4 tsp.
Mustard seeds- 1/2 tsp.
Ghee- 2 tablespoons

Oil- 2 tablespoons
A bunch of curry leaves (optional)
Salt to taste

Method:
1. Grind the ginger, peppercorns, turmeric powder, onions and green chillies to make a coarse paste.
2. Heat oil and ghee in a large pan and add mustard seeds. When it pops add cinnamon, bay leaves & cloves. When it turns brown add garlic and curry leaves.
3. After a few seconds add the onion, ginger and chilli paste. Fry for a couple of minutes. Then add the chicken pieces and fry. Add potatoes, carrots, Garam Masala and salt.
4. Cover the pan and cook for 5 minutes.
5. Then pour the coconut milk and add the green peas. Cover and cook until the chicken is fully cooked.

Chicken Do-Piaza

Ingredients:
3 lb. roasting chicken cut into bite size
6 medium onions
4 fresh green chillies, seeded
4 teaspoons chopped garlic
1 1/2 tablespoons finely grated fresh ginger
1 tablespoon ground coriander
1 tablespoon ground cumin
2 teaspoons ground turmeric
1 teaspoon ground cinnamon
1 teaspoon ground cardamom
1/4 teaspoon ground clove's
3 tablespoons ghee
3 tablespoons oil
3 ripe tomatoes, peeled and chopped
1 cup water
2 teaspoons salt

Method:
Thinly slice half the onions and set aside. Roughly chop the rest of the onions and put into electric blender with the chillies, garlic and ginger. Blend to a puree. Mix in the ground spices. Heat ghee and oil in a large saucepan and fry the sliced onions, stirring frequently, until they are golden brown. Remove onions from pan with slotted spoon. Add the blended mixture to oil remaining in pan mid fry, stirring until colour darkens and oil appears around the edges. Add tomatoes, stir and cook until liquid from tomatoes is almost evaporated. Add the chicken pieces and stir well. Add water and salt, cover and cook for 35 minutes or until chicken is

tender. Add reserved fried onions, cover and simmer 5 minutes longer. Serve with rice or parathas.

Murgh Xaguti Masala or Goan Chicken Curry

Ingredients:
2 tablespoon(s) oil
2 onions finely chopped
12 medium pieces (about 800 grams) of chicken
½ teaspoon(s) turmeric powder
2 cup(s) water
salt to taste
1 tablespoon(s) tamarind pulp
½ teaspoon(s) equal mix of mace and nutmeg powders For the Paste
1 cup(s) grated coconut
10 whole dry red Kashmiri chillies
4 cloves
2 cinnamon sticks of 1" each
2 tablespoon(s) each coriander and poppy seeds (khus khus)
1 teaspoon(s) each of black peppercorns, carom and cumin seeds
2 star anise (phoolpatri)
1 tsp garlic paste

1. Dry roast the grated coconut in a non-stick pan on low heat stirring every now and then for about 3 minutes or till it is reddish-brown and aromatic. Remove onto a plate. In the same pan dry roast all other ingredients for the paste except the garlic briefly till they turn a shade darker and give off an aroma. Grind to a paste with the coconut, garlic and water as required to make a thick fine paste.
2. Heat the oil in a thick-bottomed pan and add the onions. Sauté on medium level for about 4 minutes or till they are browned.
3. Add the chicken pieces and fry on medium-low heat for about 5 minutes or till golden on all sides.
4. Add the ground paste and turmeric powder. Fry on medium-low heat for about 5 minutes till oil separates
5. Add water, salt and mix well. Bring to a boil. Add the tamarind pulp and the mace-nutmeg powders. Cover and simmer low heat for about 12 minutes or till the chicken is fully cooked and tender.

    TIP:

6. Traditionally, chicken is cut into comparatively smaller pieces for this recipe.

Badami Murgh - Chicken Curry with One Hundred Almonds (North India)

Ingredients -
3 lb. roasting chicken
5 medium onions
2 tablespoons oil
2 tablespoons ghee
3 teaspoons finely chopped garlic
3 teaspoons finely grated fresh ginger
I tablespoon ground coriander
1 tablespoon ground cumin
1 teaspoon ground turmeric
1/2 teaspoon ground fennel
1 teaspoon chilli powder, optional
3 teaspoons salt
3 large ripe tomatoes, peeled and chopped
1/2 cup chopped fresh coriander or mint leaves
100 blanched almonds
oil for frying
1 cup yogurt
1 teaspoon Garam Masala

Method:
Cut chicken into curry pieces. Peel onions, chop 3 onions finely and slice the remaining 2 very fine. Heat ghee and oil in a large heavy saucepan and fry the 2 sliced onions, stirring, until golden brown. Remove from pan and set aside. Add the chopped onion, garlic and ginger to the oil left in pan and fry on low heat, stirring occasionally, until very soft and turning golden. Long, slow cooking at this stage is essential if the curry is to have good flavour.

Add the coriander, cumin, turmeric, fennel and chilli powder and fry, stirring, for 1-2 minutes. Add salt, tomatoes and half the fresh herbs, stir well and cook until tomatoes are pulpy. Cover pan to hasten this process, but uncover and stir now and then to ensure mixture does not stick to base of pan.

Put in the chicken pieces and stir well so that each piece is coated with the mixture. Cover pan and cook on very low heat for 40 minutes or until chicken is tender. Meanwhile heat oil and fry half the almonds until golden. Grind remaining almonds. Beat the yogurt with a fork until it is quite smooth and stir into the curry together with the fried almonds. Simmer 5 minutes, uncovered. Stir in the Garam Masala, reserved fried onions, ground almonds and remaining chopped herbs. Heat through and serve.

Moglai Murgh - Whole Chicken with Rice, Moghul Style

Ingredients
4 lb. roasting chicken
2 tablespoons almonds
1 tablespoon chironji seeds or pistachios
2 tablespoons white poppy seeds
1 teaspoon caraway seeds
1 teaspoon cumin seeds
1 teaspoon chilli powder, optional
1 teaspoon ground coriander
1/2 teaspoon ground turmeric
1/2 teaspoon saffron strands
2 tablespoons boiling water 1 cup yogurt
Salt to taste
3 hard boiled eggs
2 tablespoons ghee or oil
2 large onions, finely sliced
2 tablespoons finely chopped fresh coriander
1 tablespoon finely chopped fresh mint
2 or 3 fresh green chillies, seeded and chopped
1 cup hot water
2 cups basmati or other long grain rice
1/2 cup sultanas or raisins
1/2 cup shelled peas
Garnish:
silver leaf, optional
1/2 cup almonds or cashews, fried

Method:
Wash and dry the chicken well and with a very sharp knife make slits in the flesh of the breast, thighs and drumsticks to allow spices to penetrate.

In electric blender grind almonds, chironji or pistachios, poppy seeds, caraway and cumin. Combine these with the chilli powder, if used, and the ground coriander and turmeric. Pound saffron strands in mortar and pestle and dissolve in the boiling water, mix into yogurt together with ground spices. Add lei teaspoons salt. Rub this marinade well into the chicken, inside and out, and let it marinate for at least l hour in the refrigerator. Put the hard boiled eggs into the cavity of the chicken and truss the bird, tucking its wing tips under and tying the drumsticks together.

In a large, heavy saucepan, with a tight cover, heat the ghee or oil and fry onion until golden brown. Remove onion from pan and reserve. Scrape excess marinade from outside of chicken, put chicken in pan and fry on all sides by turning it, taking care not to let it burn. Add the marinade, coriander, mint and chillies, the fried onion and hot water. Allow to come to simmering point, cover and simmer for 40 minutes. While chicken is cooking, wash rice well and soak in cold water for 30 minutes, then drain in colander.

Carefully lift chicken from pan. Measure stock in pan and add water to make up to 4 cups if necessary. Return to pan, add remaining 2 teaspoons salt and the drained rice and bring to the boil, stirring to scrape any spice from base of pan. Put chicken on top of rice, sprinkle sultanas and peas around it, cover tightly and continue cooking for a further 30 minutes without lifting lid. Serve chicken surrounded by rice and garnished with silver leaf and fried nuts.

Chicken in a Clay Pot (Recipe conceived in The Royal Kitchens of India)

Ingredients:
3 lb. roasting chicken
1/2 teaspoon crushed garlic
1/2 teaspoon finely grated fresh ginger
1 tablespoon grated onion
1/4 teaspoon ground cardamom
1/4 teaspoon ground turmeric
1/4 teaspoon ground mace
salt to taste
1/4 teaspoon saffron strands
1 tablespoon boiling water
3 tablespoons ghee or butter
1/3 cup strong chicken stock
1 bay leaf
Stuffing:
1 tablespoon ghee of oil
1 large onion, finely chopped
1 teaspoon finely chopped garlic
3 teaspoons ground coriander
1 teaspoon ground cumin
250 g (8 oz) minced lamb
1/2 teaspoon dried fenugreek leaves, optional
1 bay leaf
1 1/2 teaspoons salt

1/2 teaspoon ground black pepper
1/4 teaspoon each ground cardamom, cinnamon and cloves
1 cup long grain rice
2 cups hot water

Method
Remove skin of chicken.
Make small slashes in the flesh of the breast, thighs and drumsticks. Combine garlic, ginger, onion, cardamom, turmeric, mace and salt. Dissolve saffron in boiling water and add. Rub the mixture well into the chicken, cover and marinate overnight in refrigerator or for at least 2 hours at room temperature.
Fill the chicken with cooked and cooled stuffing, truss the bird and place in clay casserole breast downwards. The chicken breast must be at the bottom or downwards when cooking so that the breast is immersed in stock and remains moist. Melt the ghee or butter and pour over the chicken. Pour stock into the casserole and add the bay leaf. Cover with lid so that none of the fragrant steam is lost.
Bake in a moderately slow oven 160 °C (325°F) for 2 hours or a slow oven 150C (300°F) for 4 flours if this is more convenient. Take the dish to table and uncover it there so that the guests have the experience of enjoying the aroma as it first escapes the clay casserole.
Stuffing: Heat ghee or oil and fry onion and garlic until soft and starting to turn golden. Add ground coriander and cumin and fry 1 minute, then add lamb and fry, stirring, until lamb is browned. Add all remaining ingredients except rice and water. Cover and cook on low heat for 15 minutes, stirring occasionally. Add rice and hot water, bring to a boil, stirring. Then turn heat very low, cover tightly and cook for 20-25 minutes or until liquid is absorbed by rice. Cool before using.

Butter Chicken

Ingredients:

3 lbs. chicken drumsticks/ thighs/ sliced breast pieces
1 tbsp. oil
1 tsp. ginger paste
1 tsp. garlic paste
3 tsp. chilli powder (optional)
1 cup yogurt or buttermilk
1 cup sour cream
1/2 tomato puree
4 oz. butter
6 cardamoms
6 cloves
2 sticks cinnamon
3 tsp. salt or to taste

Method:
Heat the oil in a large saucepan. Fry the ginger, garlic, cardamoms, cinnamon and cloves on medium low heat for a minute, and add the chicken with the yogurt or buttermilk, tomato puree, sour cream, chilli powder and salt. Cook on medium low heat, stirring occasionally, for half an hour, keeping the saucepan covered with a lid. Add butter before serving.

Chicken Tikka

Ingredients:
1 1/2 lbs. chicken breast; boneless and skinless
Salt; to taste
1 teaspoon Chile powder
1 teaspoon coriander seeds, ground
2 tablespoons lime juice
2 garlic cloves
1 teaspoon grated fresh ginger
2 tablespoons oil
2/3 cup yogurt
lime slices; to garnish

Method:
Rinse chicken, pat dry with paper towels and cut into 3/4.inch cubes. Thread onto short skewers. Put skewered chicken into a shallow non metal dish. In a
small bowl, mix together yogurt, ginger root, garlic, chilli powder, coriander, salt, lime juice and oil. Pour over skewered chicken and turn to coat completely
in marinade. Cover and refrigerate 6 hours or overnight to allow chicken to absorb flavours.

Heat grill. Place skewered chicken on grill rack and cook 5 to 7 minutes, turning skewers and basting occasionally with any remaining marinade. Serve hot,
garnished with lime slices.

Chicken Curry

Ingredients:

2 lb. chicken pieces
2 onions, chopped or pureed
2 tsp. ginger paste
2 tsp. garlic paste
1 tsp. turmeric powder
1 tsp. chilli powder
1 tsp. cumin powder

1 tsp. coriander powder
1 tomato, pureed
1 tsp. salt or to taste
Cilantro/coriander leaves
1 tbsp. oil

Method:
Heat oil in a saucepan and fry the onions, ginger and garlic, together with cumin and coriander powders and cilantro/coriander leaves for five minutes on low heat. Add tomato, chicken, turmeric and chilli powders and salt together with half a cup of lukewarm water and cook on medium low heat for half an hour, keeping the saucepan covered with a lid.

Silken Chicken (Murgh Makhan)

Ingredients:
1 stick butter
1 (3 lb.) chicken, skin removed and cut into 10 pieces
4 garlic cloves, halves
1 medium fresh hot green chilli, seeded
1 (2.inch) piece ginger, peeled and coarsely chopped
2 cups finely chopped onions
8 cardamom pods, cracked
9 whole cloves
2 teaspoons cumin seeds
1 teaspoon chilli powder (un-spiced ground red chills)
1 (1 1/2.inch) piece cinnamon stick
1 (16 oz.) can whole tomatoes, chopped, with juice
1/2 teaspoon salt
1/4 cup fresh coriander

Method:

Combine garlic, chilli and ginger in a blender and process for 15 seconds. Add onions and process for 15 seconds. Add cardamom pods and cloves and process for 15 seconds. Set aside.

Heat 3 tablespoons of the butter in a large skillet until the foam subsides. Over medium heat brown half the chicken pieces on all sides. Transfer to a plate. Repeat with 3 more tablespoons butter and remaining chicken.

Add remaining butter and garlic/onion/spice mixture to pan and cook, stirring constantly, for 10 minutes or until liquid has evaporated. Add cumin seeds chilli powder and cinnamon stick and cook for 2 minutes, stirring constantly. Add tomatoes, with their juice and salt.

Cook, stirring often, for 10 minutes. Add chicken and its juices. Reduce heat to low. Cook covered for 30 minutes, until chicken is tender and sauce is thickened. Garnish with fresh coriander to serve.

Tandoori Chicken

Ingredients:

10 chicken drumsticks
2 tablespoons plain yogurt
2 tablespoons tomato paste
2 tablespoons fresh ginger, shredded
6 cloves garlic, ground
2 tablespoons lemon juice
2 tablespoons vinegar
Salt, to taste
Red pepper, to taste
Garam Masala, to taste
2 tablespoons vegetable oil

Method:
Skin drumsticks and make cuts on the drumstick meat. Mix yogurt, tomato paste, ginger, garlic, lemon juice, vinegar, salt, pepper and Garam Masala. Marinate chicken in this paste for six hours. Preheat oven to 350oF and bake for 45 minutes.

FISH DISHES

Again with these dishes it is quite easy to add meat to them if you wish.

GOAN FISH CURRY

Ingredients
Fish   500 gm
Green chillies 5 gm
Onions   50 gm
Tomatoes 55 gm
Red Chillies 10 gm
Cumin seeds 20 gm
Tamarind 10 gm
Coriander 10 gm
Oil   30 ml
Coconut   115 gm

Method :
- Chop onions, Roast and grind red chillies, turmeric cumin seeds and coriander.
- Grind coconut to a fine paste. Combine all other spices.
- Fry onions in fat. Add grounded Masala and green chillies. Fry till flavour emerges.
- Add chopped tomatoes and sufficient water soak tamarind in water and extract pulp.
- Cut fish into pieces.
- When the gravy boils, add fish.
- Add tamarind pulp, curry leaves and simmer till fish is cooked.

Fish Curry with Mustard (Shorshe Maach)

Ingredients:

1 lb. fish, cut into pieces
2 tbsp. oil
1 tsp. turmeric powder
2 tbsp. mustard powder
1 tsp. salt
8 green chillies

Method:
Make a paste of mustard in an equal amount of water. Heat oil in a non stick frying pan and fry the mustard paste for half a minute, and add 3 cups of lukewarm water. Bring to a boil and add fish, turmeric and salt and green chillies. Cook on medium low heat for 30 minutes.

Prawn Patia

Ingredients:

1/2 teaspoon salt
1 teaspoon ground cumin
1 teaspoon crushed dried red chillies
4 tablespoons groundnut oil
1 capsicum, chopped small
2 large onions, sliced
1/2 oz. ginger, finely chopped

3 cloves garlic, finely chopped
4 fresh chillies, finely chopped
1 lb. prawns, peeled
1/2 teaspoon turmeric
1.14 oz. can of plum tomatoes, drained and roughly chopped
water

Method:
Heat the salt, cumin and dried chillies in a heavy frying pan over a high heat for 1 minute. Keep the spices moving. Add the oil. Lower the heat and add the onion and capsicum. Cook for a few minutes until the onions are soft.

Add the ginger, garlic and chillies. Stir for another minute. Add prawns, turmeric and tomatoes. If the mixture is too thick add a little water. Simmer until prawns are cooked through.

Shrimp Curry (Jhinka Masala)

Ingredients:
1 lb. shrimps, peeled and de-veined
1 onion, pureed
1 tsp. ginger paste
1 tsp. garlic paste
1 tomato, pureed
1 tsp. turmeric powder
1 tsp. chilli powder
1 tsp. cumin powder
1 tsp. coriander powder
1 tsp. salt or to taste
1 tsp. lemon juice
Cilantro/coriander leaves
1 tbsp. oil

Method
Heat oil in a non stick frying pan and fry the onion, tomato, ginger and garlic, together with cumin and coriander powders and cilantro/coriander leaves for five minutes on medium low heat. Add shrimp, turmeric and chilli powders and salt together with half a cup of lukewarm water and cook on medium low heat for twenty five minutes. Keep the pan covered
with a lid. Stir well to let the shrimps blend with the spices. Season with lemon juice, garnish with cilantro/coriander before serving.

VEGETABLE DISHES

Again with these dishes it is quite easy to add meat to them if you wish.

Adai

Ingredients:

Rice 1 cup
Urad Daal 1/3 cup
Chana Daal 1/3 cup
Yellow Split Peas 1/3 cup
Salt 1 tsp.
Red Chilli Powder 1 tsp.
Onion (opt.) 1 (large)
Carrot (opt.) 1
Coconut - grated (opt.) 1/4 cup

Preparation

- Mix Rice, Chana Daal, Urad Daal, and Yellow Split Peas in a large vessel. Soak in a lot of water for about 2 hours.
- Grind the soaked mixture with Chilli Power and salt coarsely, without adding much water.
- Ferment for about 3-4 hours, then refrigerate or freeze. In cold weather, the fermenting process might take longer, and it might be a good idea to ferment in an oven(the pilot light will keep the mixture warm).
- Add either onions (finely cut), carrot (grated) or coconut before preparing.

Aloo Dum

Ingredients

Oil 3 tbsp.
Bay leaf 1
Onion 1
Ginger 1/2 tsp.
Garlic 1/2 tsp.
Cumin Seeds 1/2 tsp.
Turmeric 1/4 tsp.

Chilli Powder 1 1/2 tsp.
Yogurt 2/3 tsp.
Salt 1/4 tsp.
Coriander powder 2 tsp.
Potatoes 1 lb.
Tomato 1
Capsicum 1

Preparation

- Heat oil, add bay leaf and onion. Fry for 3-4 minutes. Add ginger and garlic and fry for another minute. Add mustard and cumin seeds.
- The potatoes should be sliced, and the tomatoes and capsicum cut up. Add these, mix well, and cook for 4-5 minutes, continuously stirring.
- Sprinkle with turmeric, coriander and chilli powder.
- Beat the yogurt and blend into a smooth mixture. Add yogurt and salt.
- Mix gently, cover and cook for about 10 minutes on low heat.

Aloo Gobi

Ingredients

Cauliflower 1
Potatoes 4
Oil 1/4 cup
Cumin seeds 1 tsp.
Ginger 1 in. stick
Garlic 3 cloves
Turmeric 3/4 tsp.
Red Chilli Powder 1 tsp.
Tomatoes 3
Garam Masala 1 tsp.
Coriander powder 2 tsp.

Preparation

- Cut cauliflower into flowerets. Cube potatoes.
- Heat oil and sauté cumin seeds for about a minute. Add garlic and ginger, stir and add potatoes. Boone, add turmeric and chilli powder, and bhoona again. Add tomatoes and simmer for about 5 minutes.
- Add cauliflower and high heat for about a minutes.
- Lower heat, cover and let simmer for about 15 minutes. Curry should be damp-dry.

Aviyal

Ingredients

Mixed vets. 3 cups
Coconut (grated) 1/2 cup
Green/Red Chillies 2 - 3
More Kozhambhu powder 2 tsp.
Yogurt 2 cups

Preparation

- Boil vegetables for about 5 minutes.
- Add yogurt and powder to vegetables.
- Bring to boil.

Chole

Ingredients

Garbanzo beans(or Chick Peas) 1 tin
Onion 1
Ginger 1 tsp.
Garlic 1 tsp.
Tomatoes 1/2 can
Cumin powder 1 tsp.
Coriander powder 1 tsp.
Chilli powder 1 tsp.
Tamcom 1/2 tsp.
Garam Masala 1 tsp.
Coriander Leaves bunch

Preparation

- Sauté onions, add garlic and ginger. Fry for about 5 minutes.
- Add tomatoes, and continue frying.
- Add cumin, coriander and chilli powders, and some salt. Fry for another 5 minutes.
- Add garbanzo beans (or chick peas), boil for a few minutes.

- Add Garam Masala, let mixture simmer.
- Separately, boil tamcon in water until it dissolves. Add this to main mixture.
- Remove from stove. Serve garnished with coriander leaves and lemon slices.

Beans/Potato Curry

Ingredients

Oil 2 tbsp.
Mustard seeds 1 tsp.
Urad Daal 1 tsp.
Veg. 3 cups
Salt to taste
Turmeric pinch

Preparation

- Heat oil, mustard seeds, and Urad Daal. Roast for a few seconds.
- Add vegetables. Sprinkle salt and turmeric. Cook on high heat for a couple of minutes.
- Add coriander powder, chilli powder, and cumin powder, (and ginger and garlic if you wish) cover and cook on low until done.
- For making the potatoes crisper, add rice powder (arshi maav) and stir it in.

Cabbage Curry

Ingredients

Oil 2 tbsp.
Mustard seeds 1 tsp.
Urad Daal 1 tsp.
Cumin seeds 1 tsp.
Green Chilli 1
Mixed vegetables. 1 cup
Cabbage 1 medium size
Salt to taste
Turmeric pinch

Preparation

- Heat oil, mustard seeds, Urad Daal, cumin seeds, and green chilli. Roast for a few seconds.
- Add mixed vegetables. and cabbage. Sprinkle salt and turmeric. Cook on high heat for a couple of minutes, then cover and cook on low until done.

Daal

Ingredients

Arhar/Toor Daal 1 cup
Tomato 1
Onion 1
Turmeric pinch
Salt to taste
Bay Leaf (optional) 2-3
Coriander powder 1/2 tsp.
Chilli powder 1/4 tsp.

Preparation

- Cook Arhar Daal in 3 cups of water. Bring to boil and remove foam.
- Add bay leaves, turmeric, and a few drops of oil, and continue to boil.
- Cook daal until soft and then mash mixture.
- Fry onions, coriander and chilli powders together, and add to daal.
- Add cut tomato and salt, and heat for a couple of minutes more.

Dosai

Ingredients

Rice 1 1/2 cups
Urad Daal 1/2 cup
Salt 2 tsp.

Preparation

- Soak the rice and daal separately in slightly warm water for 2 - 8 hours.
- Grind separately to a smooth paste and mix in a large vessel with salt. Mix thoroughly (use blender if possible).
- Ferment for 12 hours.

Gajar Halva

Ingredients

Carrots 1 lb.
Half and Half 1 pint
Sugar 1_2cup
Cardamom 3-4
Raisins handful
Cashew nuts handful

Preparation

- Add a little butter to a frying pan and heat to coat the pan. Roast cashew nuts until golden brown and add the raisins to the pan for a few seconds. Remove the cashews and raisins and keep aside.
- Grate the carrots and add to the pan. Add Half and Half, and heat for about an hour, starting with high heat stirring, and lowering the heat after the mixture starts boiling. Heat until almost dry.
- Add sugar, mix, and continue to cook until damp/dry.
- Remove from stove and add cashews and raisins and cardamoms.

Kootu

Masala Ingredients

Urad Daal 2 tsp.
Black pepper 1/3 tsp.
Red Chillies 2
Cumin Seeds 1 tsp.
Coconut (grated) 3 tbsp.

Masala Preparation

- Roast Urad Daal, Black Pepper and Red Chillies until the Daal is golden yellow.
- Add Cumin seeds to the mixture after removing from stove.
- Add the coconut when the mixture is cold. Grind with water.

Ingredients

Yellow Split Peas 1/2 cup
Chilli powder 1/4 tsp.
Turmeric pinch
Spinach 10 oz.
or
Vegetables etc. 4 - 5 cups

Preparation

- Boil Yellow Split Peas. Keep aside.
- Boil vegetables(spinach or combo of cabbage, squash, beans, etc.) with salt, chilli powder and turmeric until just cooked.
- Add Masala and daal.

Masur Daal

Ingredients

Masur Daal 1 cup
Onion 1
Ginger 1 in.
Water 3 1/2 cup
turmeric pinch
garlic 2 cloves
cumin seeds 1 tsp.
butter 2 tbsp.

Preparation

- Wash well the daal and drain it.
- Boil the water and add the daal, salt, pepper, turmeric, finely chopped ginger, and garlic. Cover the pot and simmer for 20 min's.
- When done, heat the ghee add the cumin. Fry till golden brown and add thinly sliced onions. Fry till crisp and brown.

May add paprika and finely chopped tomatoes to the above for colour. Pour over the daal and serve.

Molahu Kozhambhu

Masala Ingredients

Black Pepper 1 tsp.
Red chillies 6
Chana Daal 1 tbsp.
Toor Daal 1 tbsp.
Coriander Seeds 1 tbsp.
Coconut(grated) 1 tbsp.

Masala Preparation

- Fry all ingredients (except coconut) in as little oil as possible.
- Add coconut, grind (very fine) in blender.

Ingredients

Tamcon 1 flat tsp.
Salt 2 tsp.
Mustard Seeds 1 tsp.
Turmeric pinch
Tomatoes 1/2 can
Rice powder 1 tsp.
Hing 1/4 tsp.

Preparation

- Heat oil, mustard seeds.
- Add 4 cups water, tamcon, Masala, turmeric, tomatoes, and salt to the pan. Boil for about 10 minutes.
- Add asafoetida, rice powder and stir to thicken. Boil for another minute or so.

More Kozhambhu

Ingredients

Yogurt 32 oz.
Coriander seeds 2 tsp.
Cumin seeds 2 tsp.
Red Chilli powder 1 tsp.
Chana Daal 1 tsp.

Rice or rice powder 1 tsp.
Coconut (grated) 2 tsp.
Salt 2 tsp.
Mustard 1 tsp.
Turmeric pinch
Red Chilli 1

Preparation

- Fry Coriander seeds, Cumin seeds, Chana Daal, Red Chilli in a little oil.
- Grind the mixture with the coconut and add to the beaten yogurt. Add turmeric and bring to a boil.
- Stir in rice powder, and heat on low until consistent texture is achieved.
- Heat oil and mustard seeds and add to the mixture.

Navarattan Curry

Ingredients

Potato 1 large
Random vegetables 4 cups
Butter 2 tbsp.
Onion 1 large
Garlic 2 cloves
Tomatoes 2
Yogurt 2 tbsp.
Heavy cream 1/2 cup
Green peas 4 oz
Raisins 1/4 cup
Blanched almonds 12

Dry Masala Ingredients

Cardamom (ground) 1/2 tsp. Coriander powder 1/2 tsp. Ginger (ground) 1/2 tsp. Red Chilli powder 1/2 tsp. Turmeric 1/2 tsp. Note: For the random vegetables, can use, e.g., broccoli, green peppers, carrots, cauliflower, green beans, etc.

Preparation

- Boil vegetables (except onions and peas). Drain and set aside.
- Melt butter and sauté onions and garlic. Add tomatoes, yogurt, and the dry Masala, and simmer for 5 minutes. Add vegetables and simmer for another 5 minutes, then add water. Cover and simmer for 10 minutes. Add cream and peas, stirring gently.

- Before serving, top with raisins and almonds.

Rajma

Ingredients

Red Kidney Bean 2 cup
turmeric pinch
oil 1/4 cup
ginger 1 in.
tomatoes 3
water 3 quarts
salt 1 tsp.
onion 1
Garam Masala 1 tsp.
Coriander Leaves small bunch

Preparation

- Wash beans and boil for 2 - 3 hours or 1/2 hour in pressure cooker.
- In the meantime make Masala of onions, garlic, ginger and tomato as in ? curry.
- Add to the beans and cook again till most of the liquid dries up and the beans are soft and thoroughly cooked.
- Garnish with coriander leaves and serve.

Ras Malai

Ingredients

Ricotta Cheese 2 lb.
Half and Half 2 qts.
Sugar 2 cups
Cardamom pods 5
Bay leaf 1
Vanilla 1 tsp.
Rose Water To taste (opt.)

Preparation

- Mix 1.5 cups of sugar with the Ricotta cheese and bake it in a 400o F oven for about 1hr and 15 minutes in a flat dish covered with aluminium foil. The cheese should have hardened and turned a pale brown.
- Thicken the Half and Half by simmering over low heat for a long time. This is best done in a microwave; if a microwave is not available, do it over low heat and stir frequently. Thicken until the volume drops to around half of the original volume.
- Add the remaining 0.5 cup sugar, cardamom pods, bay leaf, vanilla and rose water (and any other flavouring that you may want) to the Half and Half. Heat for a few minutes.
- After the cheese has been baked, cut it into 1 inch squares and add to the hot thickened half and half. Cool for a few hours in the fridge.

Rasagolla

Ingredients

Milk 1 gallon
Lemon Juice 1 cup
Sugar 1 cup

Preparation

- Bring one gallon of milk to a boil. When boiling add one cup of either whiter vinegar or lemon juice. Turn the stove off. Milk should separate into whey and curd.
- Pour into colander, leaving only the panir/curd. Leave curd in strainer until cold and dry. This will take at least an hour (you can leave it overnight).
- Place curd in food processor and process for one minute. It should be soft but not sticky.
- Form small balls from the curd. Using vinegar usually results in about 80 to 100 rasagollas.
- Bring one cup sugar and 3 cups water to a boil in a pressure cooker. Place 20-25 rasagollas in syrup. Turn off the heat to place the cover on the pressure cooker. Turn heat on high. When cooker begins to whistle wait for a couple of minutes, then turn it off.
- When pressure cooker depressurizes, remove cover and re-peat previous step with the rest of the rasagollas. Do not use the same sugar syrup more than once.

Rasam

Ingredients

Tomatoes 2
Turmeric Powder 1/4 tsp.
Tamcon (or tamarind paste) 1 1/2 tsp.
Toor Daal 3/4 cup
Ghee 1 tsp.
Mustard seeds 1 tsp.
Coriander leaves bunch

Preparation

- Boil tamcon in water.
- Boil toor daal in water.
- Cut tomatoes, add to tamcon solution. Add asafoetida and salt. Boil for a couple of minutes.
- Add mashed toor daal and rasam Masala.
- In a pan, heat ghee, fry mustard seeds.
- Add fresh coriander leaves and mustard seeds.

Rasam Masala

Masala Ingredients

Black Pepper 1 tbsp.
Chana Daal seeds 2 tbsp.
Coriander Seeds 2 tbsp.
Red Chillies 4-5
Asafoetida(optional) 1 tsp.
Coconut (grated) 3 tbsp.
Ghee 2 tbsp.

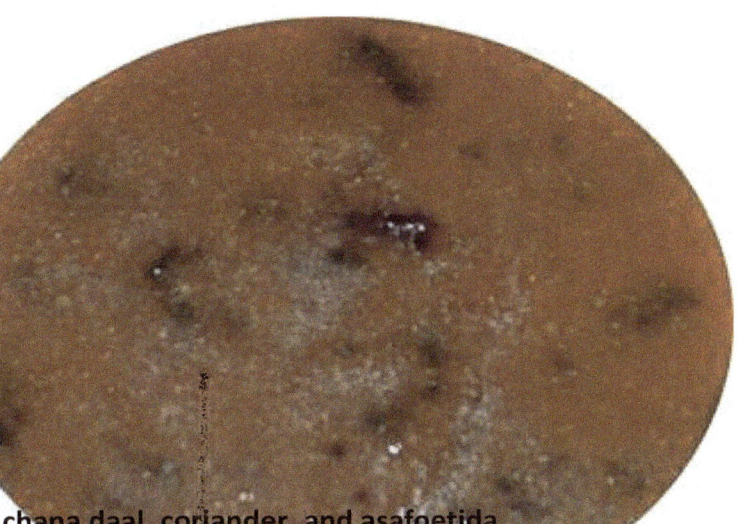

Masala Preparation

- Roast black pepper, chana daal, coriander, and asafoetida.
- Add chillies when daal starts getting red.
- If using dry coconut, soak it in a little water. Blend the daal mixture and coconut until the paste is fine. Keep aside.

Sambar

Ingredients

Tamcon 1 tbsp.
Mustard Seeds 1 tbsp.
Vegetables as needed
Turmeric pinch
Salt to taste
Toor Daal 1 cup
Curry Leaves 2-3
Ghee 2 tsp.

Preparation

- Boil toor daal and mash.
- Boil tamcon in water until dissolved.
- Take the vegetables, slightly fry them, and add them to this tamarind water. Add a little salt and turmeric and boil.
- When vegetables are soft, add the toor daal paste and wait until the mixture boils again. Lower flame.
- Add curry leaves, the Masala mixture, salt and boil for a few minutes, stirring occasionally.

Optional: Garnish with roasted mustard seeds.
Note: If the toor daal gets burnt, rectify by adding a small ball of cooked rice (it will remove the odour). It will also absorb excess salt, so compensate for this when eating.

Sambar Masala

Masala Ingredients

Methi (Fenugreek) 1 tsp.
Chana Daal seeds 2 tbsp.
Coriander Seeds 4 tbsp.
Red Chillies 4-5
Asafoetida(optional) 1 tsp.
Coconut (grated) 3 tbsp.
Oil 2 tbsp.

Masala Preparation

- Roast methi, chana daal, and asafoetida.
- Add chillies when daal starts getting red.
- If using dry coconut, soak it in a little water and blend the daal mixture and coconut until the paste is fine. Keep aside.

Sooji Halwa

Ingredients

Rava 1 cup
Water 3 cups
Sugar 1 1/2 cups
Ghee 3-4 tbsp.
Cardamoms few
Cashews some
Raisins some
Saffron/Turmeric pinch

Preparation

- Roast rava until light brown.
- Boil 3 cups of water, add sugar, and allow it to completely dissolve.
- Add rava to water slowly, stirring.
- Fry cardamoms, raisins, cashews in ghee. Add to rava.
- Add saffron/turmeric and mix.

Uppuma

Ingredients

Oil 2 tbsp.
Water 3 cups
Onion 1
Rava 2 cups
Mixed vegetables. 1 cup
Mustard seeds 1 tsp.
Urad Daal 1 tsp.

Chana Daal 1 tsp.
Ginger 1 tsp.
Green chillies 2
Red Chilli 1

Preparation

- Roast rava until light brown.
- Separately, fry mustard seeds, urad and chana daals, chopped onion, (crushed) red and (chopped) green chillies in oil. (Optional: can add cumin and coriander powders, peas, mixed vegetables, etc. and fry these too.)
- Add water to the fried mixture, bring it to a boil, lower the flame, and add the rava slowly, stirring while doing so.
- Optional: add cashews.

Vada

Ingredients

Moong Daal 1/2 cup
Urad Daal 1/2 cup
Onion 1
Coriander 2 tsp.
Green Chilli 1
Chilli powder 1/2 tsp.
Salt 1 tsp.
Ginger 1 tsp.
Baking Soda 1/4 tsp.

Preparation

- Soak urad daal and moong daal for 2-3 hours.
- Grind daals into a coarse paste.
- Add finely chopped onion, salt, coriander powder, chilli powder OR green chilli, ginger and soda. Mix well and set aside for 4-5 minutes.
- Fry small spoonfuls of the mixture in hot oil.

Vegetable Jalfrasie

Onion 1 large
Green peppers 2
Tomatoes 2 large
Broccoli 1/2 lb.
Cauliflower 1/2 lb.
Butter 4 tbsp.
Red Chilli Powder 1 tsp.
Turmeric 1/2 tsp.
Ginger 1 in. stick
Garlic 3 cloves
White vinegar 2 tbsp.
Tomato puree 2 tbsp.

Preparation

- Chop onion; cut green peppers, tomatoes, broccoli, and cauliflower into 1 in. cubes.
- Melt butter and sauté onion. Add all the remaining vegetables and stir-fry for about 5 minutes over medium heat.
- Add the spices and vinegar. Stir in the tomato puree, and simmer for about 5 minutes. Season to taste with salt and fresh-ground pepper.

Vellirikkai Thogayal

Ingredients

1 large or 2 medium cucumbers
3 tbspn oil (sesame, if you have it)
1 tspn black mustard seeds
1 tspn white urad dal
1/2 tspn fenugreek (methi)
2-4 dried red chillies
1/2 tbsp tamcon paste
a good pinch asafoetida
salt to taste.

Preparation

- Peel cucumber, slit into half, scoop out seeds. Slit into further narrow strips and cut tiny pieces as for kachumbar. Should not be grated as this gives no 'bite' feel in the mouth.
- Next, warm the oil and fry all ingredients except the tamarind. Mustard should stop spluttering and dal/methi should turn brown. Drain out these fried spices into a blender, leaving oil behind in pan.
- Add cucumber and stir fry for two min's, no more.
- Add tamcon to spices in blender and with half the cucumber run on low speed till everything looks coarsely ground and blended. Remove into a bowl, add remaining cucumber pieces and mix well.

Pulikacchal

Ingredients

Soaked tamarind about the size of a large lemon
1 1/2 tbspn jaggery
2 tbspn sesame seeds roasted dry
6-8 green chillies, slit into two (add more for spice)
2 inch ginger cut into thin strips
1 tspn mustard seeds
1 tspn chana dal
3-4 tbspn oil, preferably sesame
good pinch asafoetida
pinch turmeric
curry leaves

Preparation

- Squeeze out the pulp from the tamarind. You can add a little fresh water each time to extract the pulp. When you have a about a small bowl full, set aside.
- Warm oil, season with mustard seeds first. When they start to pop throw in red chillies, chana dal, and asafoetida and curry leaves. When dal turns red, add the green chillies and fry. Throw in the ginger, add tamarind extract carefully, a pinch turmeric, salt to taste and jaggery. Simmer on low heat till raw smell disappears and the sauce has reduced to one-third or thickened yet spoonable.
- Crush the roasted sesame seeds with a rolling pin on paper or in a spice mill rather coarsely. Add this at the end to the pulikacchal Mix well so there are no lumps.

Gotsu

Ingredients

One small to medium eggplant
1/2 tbsp tamarind paste or extract from a tamarind size marble, soaked
one large onion, chopped (if using little ones in a bag, about five)
2 ripe tomatoes, diced
6 hot green chills, slit and cut into pieces
curry leaves
1 tspn mustard
1/2 tspn turmeric
garlic (optional)
salt to taste
3-4 tbspn oil

Preparation

- Chop the eggplant into very tiny pieces. Heat oil, add mustard seeds, when popping add curry leaves, chillies, onions and fry till onions become translucent. Add tomatoes and eggplant and fry for another five minutes. If using tamarind paste add a cup and half of water, or pour equal quantity of extract from fresh pulp. Throw in the turmeric, salt and garlic. Let it simmer for a while until eggplant becomes really soft and is barely able to retain its shape. Remove from heat.
- Tomato-Onion Gotsu More tomatoes can be substituted instead of the eggplant for a tomato- onion gotsu. Add more chillies if necessary.

Katirikka Rasavangi

Ingredients

One Bhima eggplant(Brinjal)
1/2 tbsp tamarind paste
1 1/2 tspn coriander seeds
1 tspn chana dal
3-4 dried red chillies
4 tbsp coconut (dry will do but fresh is better)
1/2 cup cooked toovar dal (with turmeric)
1/2 tspn mustard seeds
a pinch asafoetida
curry leaves

A little oil for roasting and seasoning
salt to taste

Preparation

- Cube eggplant. In about a cup of water dissolve the tamcon paste. Set on stove, add eggplant to tamarind water, a little turmeric, salt and let cook until eggplant is done but has not lost its shape.
- In a pan with very little oil roast red chillies, coriander seeds, chana dal and asafoetida. When you can get the aroma of roasted coriander or the red chillies have turned a dark, dark red remove from heat and let cool. Throw into blender with coconut, add 3 tbsp water and grind slowly into paste. Add a little water if blade gets stuck. Remove from jar and wash it out with water and save this.
- Mash cooked dal with a spoon until blended and add to cooked eggplant. Now add the coconut paste and its water. Keep on low heat till it starts to simmer a little. Take off heat.
- Season with spluttering mustard seeds and curry leaves.
- Variations: You can throw in a handful of chick peas from a can into this, thin it out somewhat and have it as katirikka sambar. Alternately, you can make the cooked dal with half toor and half chana dal, in which case you should not cook until mashed. Remove a trifle before it gets fully done.

Eggplant (Brinjal) curry with coriander

Preparation

- Get certain amount of brinjals [the long thin ones, or the short small ones found in the Indian stores are recommended-though the Bhima Brinjal aka Eggplant found in grocer. is also fine].
- Cut the Brinjals to long thin pieces [to get an idea for the size: for the long thin Indian ones, I slice them vertically into four quadrants, and horizontally into 2-3 cylinders.]
- Keep the brinjal aside.
- Get certain amount of coriander [for one small bhima brinjal, I use about 1 coriander bunch] and 1-2 green chillies. Put them in blender, add some water and blend it into watery paste.
- Now, in a large pan, heat 2-3 tb. spoons of Vitamin E (Oil), and add black grams [urad daal/minapa pappu] mustard seeds, dry red chillies (in that order) and fry them.
- When they are being fried, add the brinjal pieces to the seasoning, and cook for 6-7 minutes in medium heat (while stirring the brinjal pieces).

- First, Add salt along with the coriander/chilly paste Next, add the coriander/chilly watery paste to the brinjals. Cover the pan partially and cook in medium/low heat.
- Second, cook until the brinjal soaks up the coriander paste, but doesn't become too soft and crumbly
- At the end, add some tamarind water [you may also add flour if the curry is too watery for your taste].
- The curry is now ready.

Vankaya Kaaram Petti Koora

Preparation

- Make the curry in the same way as above (step 1-3, 5, 6, 8 are same) but instead of coriander/green chilly paste, put the "Kaaram" made as follows: In a small pan, roast (with very little oil), 3-4 tb spoons of split chana daal (Bengal grams), 2-3 tb. spoons of urad daal (black grams), 2 tb. sp. of whole Dhaniya (coriander) seeds, 1 tea spoon mustard seeds, 2-3 small dry red chillies, and (optionally) 0.5 tb. spoon of white sesame seeds. Dry grind the roasted mixture into powder (it is actually better to stop grinding when you have small pieces of chana daal). Add this powder to the brinjal in step above.

Didir Onion Rava Dosa

Ingredients

one cup semolina/rava
one cup maida
1/2 cup rice flour
4-5 green chillies finely chopped
3/4 inch ginger chopped fine
1 1/2 tspn jeera slightly crushed (enough to bring out its flavour)
salt to taste
good pinch asafoetida
2-3 chopped onions
a bunch cashews
oil to make dosas

Preparation

- Mix rava, maida, rice flour together into a thick batter adding little water at a time so no lumps are formed. Mixing by hand is a good idea if you don't have a whisk or electric mixer. Add salt, crushed cumin asafoetida and leave in a warm spot for six to seven hours at least.
- When ready to eat, spray a non-stick pan lightly with oil and warm.
- Thin out the batter to the consistency where it can be drizzled onto the pan with a spoon. Drop chopped green chillies and ginger into batter.
- Sprinkle some of the cut onions and cashews onto the pan and now continuing on low-medium heat, drizzle the batter such that there is a lattice work effect. A lot of holes is just the thing. Dribble a bit of oil around it and when the edges start turning brown coax it off the pan with a flat, wide spatula and flip it over. Remove in a few minutes and make more.
- For the plain rava dosa leave out the onions.

Didir Dosa

Ingredients

3 measures of rice flour
1 measure of urad flour

Preparation

- Mix well so no lumps are formed. Salt to taste. Leave covered in a large pot overnight. Make thin crepes, preferably in non-stick pan.

Pesarattu

Ingredients

1 cup mung dal
1/3 cup rice
4 green chillies

1 tspn cumin
1 inch piece ginger
salt to taste
oil for making dosas
1 cup chopped onions
chopped coriander

Preparation

- Soak mung dal and rice five to six hours. Grind to rava consistency with chillies, ginger and cumin. Add chopped onions, coriander and mix well without beating. Lay out thin crepes in non-stick pan and do same as for regular dosas.

Onion Vetha Kozhambu

Ingredients

lemon size tamarind soaked in about a cup of water
pearl onions/shallots peeled
2 dried red chilli pods
1 1/2 tspn sambar powder
1 1/2 tspn rice flour mixed with a little water for thickening
salt to taste
mustard, chana dal, curry leaves for seasoning
a pinch asafoetida
2 tbspn oil

Preparation

- Warm oil. Season with mustard, chana dal and curry powder. Sauté peeled onions till translucent. Add squeezed out extract of tamarind. Throw the sambar powder, salt and asafoetida in. Let simmer till onions are cooked. Add dissolved rice flour water for thickening. Stir and wait till it simmers again a couple of minutes. Remove
- Variations: Tomatoes with chick peas makes a delicious vatha kozhambu. Add some slit green chillies if you would like to spike it up. Other suggestions are diced sweet potato, diced butternut squash, daikon (Chinese radish), drumsticks (available fresh in Indian stores or canned, pre-cooked) all on their own.

Pitlai

Ingredients

2 med bitter gourds ("karela")
3/4 can chickpeas
1/2 cup cooked toovar dal
3 green chillies slit
1 1/2 tspn tamarind paste
3-4 red dry chillies
2 tspn urad dal
1 1/2 tspn coriander seeds
1/2 cup grated coconut
few peppercorns
a little jaggery or sugar
turmeric, salt to taste
mustard seeds, curry leaves, oil for seasoning

Preparation

- Slit bitter gourd into four quarters and cut 1/2 inch thick pieces across.
- In a little oil, sauté cut bitter gourd and green chillies. Add 2 cups water, tamarind, turmeric and salt. Let simmer until bitter gourd are tender. Add chickpeas and jaggery/sugar.
- While bitter gourd are cooking, in another pan sprinkle a little oil and fry coriander seeds, urad dal, red chillies and peppercorns until well roasted. Add coconut, stir a min or two and then grind in a blender. Add a little tomato paste if handy for colour.
- Blend in coconut paste into the bitter gourd-tamarind mixture. Add the dal. Mix well and reheat a till it begins to simmer. Take off stove.
- Pour seasoning on top.

Cabbage, potatoes and peas molagootal

Ingredients

1/2 cup mung dal
1/2 a small head cabbage chopped fine
1 large baking potato, diced
a bunch frozen peas
1 heaped tspn sambar powder
turmeric, salt to taste
shredded dry coconut (fine variety) soaked in a little water
mustard, urad dal, dry red chilli, curry leaves and oil for seasoning

Preparation

- Set dal to cook in about 2 cups water and a touch turmeric. When dal is three-quarters done add shredded cabbage, potatoes and a little more water if needed on top of the dal. Add sambar powder and salt.
- Cover with a lid and let it simmer away another 10 to 15 min's. Veggies should be done but still holding their shape. Stir in wet coconut. Remove from heat. Top with seasoning as explained in previous recipes.
- If more particular, grind fresh coconut with roasted red chilli and roasted urad dal paste in lieu of the desiccated coconut.
- Variations: You can do a keerai (spinach) kootan with a little modification. Add fresh coconut ground with roasted red chillies, urad dal and a little cumin. Also you can cook toovar dal separately or throw veggies + dal in a cooker for a few minutes, if you like. This tends to overcook veggies but can be done fast.

Vangi bath

Ingredients

1 medium sized eggplant;
Coriander seeds,
asafoetida,
dried red chilli (2/3/4),
urad dal, turmeric,
cinnamon sticks.
Basmati (or plain) rice, cooked.
Coconut - shredded (the large-shredded variety preferred over the micro-shredded type)
1 large lemon

Preparation

- Cook the rice. The usual way - but to get it dry, fluffy and light (not at all sticky)..
- Skin the eggplant and chop it into cubes; sprinkle lemon juice on the cubes (+ some salt) and let sit for 30 min's or so.
- In a large saucepan, heat some oil and when hot, toss the spices in and fry for 2-3 min's.. When the colour had changed dark, use a slotted spoon and toss the contents into a plate lined with a paper napkin (this will drain out the oil sticking to the spices).

- Add some oil to the pan and when hot, toss the coconut in and keep stirring until the coconut becomes brown/golden. Remove in a manner similar to the spices.
- To the pan, add some oil and when hot, add the soaked eggplant cubes and stir until 75
- Remove the eggplant and keep in a warm container.
- In a blender (or coffee grinder), blend the spices and coconut until you have a powder.
- In a pot, boil 1/4th cup water, lots of lemon juice, 1/2 tsp turmeric and some salt.
- Into the cooked rice, toss the contents of the pot and stir. The rice should take on the colour of the turmeric.
- Now, add the contents of the blender. The rice should take the colour of the spice-mix and here and there, you can see a glimpse of the yellow turmeric colour.
- Squeeze lemon onto the eggplant; let sit for 1-2 min's; toss the eggplant into the rice and stir.
- Taste a bit; if you need salt, add. If you feel something is missing, squeeze some lemon, stir and repeat. (You may choose to add some salt that way too) Vangi bath is ready. Serve with yogurt raita/pachadi.

Venn pongal

Ingredients

2 cups rice 3/4 cup mung dal,
dry roasted to a golden brown cracked black peppercorns
1 1/2 tspn lightly crushed cumin, turmeric,
salt to taste. A good bunch curry leaves
a little chopped ginger
5-6 tbspn ghee/melted butter turned brown
bunch cashews

Preparation

- Wash rice and roasted dal. Add water to one inch above level of rice. Add turmeric and let it simmer. Add a little more water if not semi-solid. When done remove from heat.
- Warm ghee and roast cashews until a golden, remove carefully and set aside. Throw in cumin seeds, cracked pepper, curry leaves into the ghee and in a minute or two pour onto the pongal with the cashews. Add the ginger. Mix well.

Vegetable Biryani

Ingredients

2 1/2 cups rice (basmati preferred)
2 med-large onions, chopped fine
To soak: in 2 cups thick yogurt, good if homemade with half and half)
FOR BEST RESULTS: soak for 2-3 hours.
6 med tomatoes, diced, 6 cardamoms, 6 cloves
6 cinnamon sticks, 1 tspn turmeric
1 tspn Garam Masala
2 tspn Dhania powder
1/2 tspn red chilli powder
1 bunch chopped coriander
1 bunch chopped fresh mint
5 green chillies, slit
Grind to paste: (and add to above yogurt mix to soak)
4-5 cloves garlic, 4 green chillies,
inch ginger.

Preparation

Fry half the onions in a little ghee/oil until translucent, add washed drained rice, stir till oil coated and a little crisp. Cook on low, low heat till 3/4 quarters done. Remove from heat.

- Sliver veggies. (carrots, beans) (cauliflower in small florets)
- Warm 4 tbspn oil and a little ghee for flavour. Drop bay leaves, fennel, star anise (a must!). Fry onions till clear. Add veggies, stir until crisp cooked. Add yogurt mix. Salt to taste. And cook it down till thick and spoonable.
- Pre-heat oven to 400.
- Spread some rice in a large aluminium baking pan, then alternate by spreading some of the yogurt mix. Repeat alternating rice and yogurt mix till everything is used up. Cover tightly with foil wrap by crimping foil over edges of pan. Bake for 30 min's.

Badusha

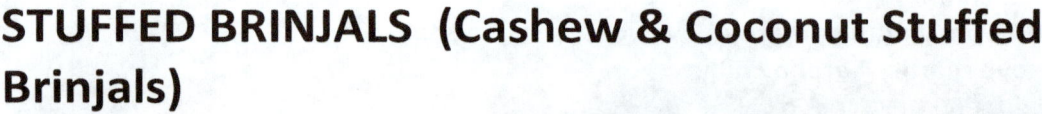

Ingredients

2 cups bisquick, sour cream, 2 cups sugar, 1 cup water

Preparation

- Make one thread consistency syrup with sugar and water.
- Make a dough with bisquick and sour cream. Roll it into balls and flatten slightly. Score a circle on the patty with a knife or small cap.
- Deep fry in crisco or oil on low fire till a med brown.
- Dip in syrup by pushing it deep down, remove and set aside. Can place a walnut or pecan in the centre immediately after dipping.

STUFFED BRINJALS (Cashew & Coconut Stuffed Brinjals)

INGREDIENTS
8 small, round brinjals,
2 cups scrapped coconut,
1 cup broken cashew nuts,
4 large onions, ¼ cup tamarind juice,
4 round potatoes,
1 tsp chilli powder,
½ tsp turmeric powder,
1 tsp mixed spices (powdered cloves, cardamom & pepper),
8 peppercorns,
6 cloves,
1 tbsp coriander seeds,
½ cup oil,
salt to taste,
1 cup chopped coriander leaves.

METHOD
Remove stems & slit brinjals crosswise without cutting all the way through. Peel potatoes but leave whole. Slice two onions. Heat two tbsp oil & fry peppercorns, cloves & coriander seeds. When they pop, add sliced onions. Brown. Add scraped coconut & roast till golden. Cool & grind to a fine paste, adding very little water. Add to this paste the chilli powder, turmeric, mixed spice, salt, tamarind juice, coriander leaves & the remaining two onions chopped very finely. Add cashew nuts & mix well. Stuff this mixture into the brinjals. Heat remaining oil in a heavy

pan. Add the brinjals, potatoes & remaining coconut paste. Add just enough water to cook the vegetables on a low, even fire.

Aviyal - Mixed Vegetables with Coconut (Kerala)

This is one of the most popular ways of serving vegetables in South India.

Ingredients:
About 6 cups mixed vegetables cut into julienne strips- carrots, French beans, zucchini, pumpkin, capsicum, eggplant, choko, cucumber, etc.
1/2 cup fresh green peas
1/2 cup freshly grated coconut or 3 tablespoons desiccated coconut
1 cup water
1 teaspoon cumin seeds
1 teaspoon chopped garlic
2 fresh green chillies, seeded
1/2 cup thick coconut milk
Salt to taste
6 curry leaves

Method:
In a saucepan bring to the boil enough lightly salted water to cover one kind of vegetable. Boil each vegetable separately, just long enough to make it tender but not soft and mushy. Take out vegetables on slotted spoon and put them in a bowl. Use the same water for all the vegetables, adding a little water at a time as it boils away, but keeping the quantity small. Save the cooking liquid.
In a blender put the coconut, water, cumin seeds, garlic and chillies. Blend on high speed until the coconut is very finely ground. Put this into the saucepan with the vegetable stock, add the coconut milk, salt and curry leaves and bring to the boil. Add the vegetables, simmer uncovered for 5 minutes. Serve hot with rice.

Potato Lasan Kari - Potato Garlic Curry (Tamil Nadu)
Serves: 4

Ingredients:
12 oz small potatoes

5 oz whole garlic cloves peeled
8-10 small onions, preferably red onions peeled
8 large fresh mild chillies with seeds removed
2 tablespoons vegetable oil
1 teaspoon fenugreek seeds
1 teaspoon chilli powder
1/2 teaspoon ground turmeric
1.5 cups coconut milk
salt to taste
2 teaspoons tamarind pulp or 1/2 teaspoon instant tamarind
'/4 cup hot water

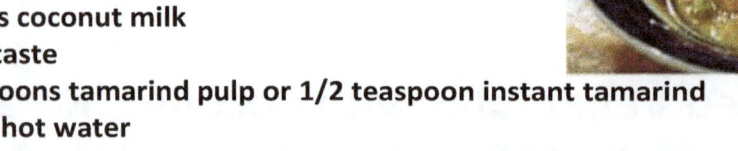

Method:
Heat oil in a heavy saucepan and fry the garlic, onions and chillies over gentle heat, not letting them brown too much. Remove from pan. Add fenugreek seeds to the oil in pan and stir over low heat just until they are golden. Add the chilli powder and turmeric and potato, fry for a few seconds, then add the coconut milk, salt and stir while bringing slowly to simmering point. Return the garlic, onions and chillies and allow to simmer, uncovered, until garlic cloves and potato are soft, about 30 minutes depending on size. Meanwhile dissolve tamarind in hot water, strain into curry for last 10 minutes of cooking. Serve with hot white rice.

Aloo Began - Vegetarian

1 lb. potatoes (Aloo)
1 lb. eggplant (began)
2 medium onions, chopped
1/4 tablespoon ginger paste or powder
1/4 teaspoon garlic paste or powder
2 medium tomatoes
1/4 teaspoon cumin powder
1/4 teaspoon turmeric powder
1/4 teaspoon coriander powder
Salt to taste
3 tablespoon oil
1/2 cup chopped cilantro

Directions:
Cut potatoes, eggplant and tomatoes in small cubes.
Heat the oil in a pan. Fry the onion for 1 minute. Add garlic, ginger, cumin, turmeric and coriander; mix together for 2 minutes. Add potato and eggplant, and cook for 13 to 15 minutes. Add tomato, and cook for 3 minutes. Sprinkle with cilantro.
Serve hot with naan, pita bread or rice.

Chickpea Curry (Chole Masala)

1 lb. canned chickpeas
1 large potato, cooked and cubed
1 tbsp. oil
1 large onion, pureed
1 large tomato, pureed
1 tsp. ginger paste
1 tsp. garlic paste
1/2 tsp. each cumin, coriander, turmeric and chilli powders.
1 tsp. salt or to taste
Cilantro/coriander leaves

Directions:
Heat oil in a non-stick frying pan (or skillet) and fry the onion and tomato, ginger and garlic pastes, cumin, coriander, turmeric and chilli powders together for a couple of minutes. Add the potatoes and chickpeas and 1/2 cup of lukewarm water and cook until done. Garnish with cilantro/coriander leaves.

Green Moong Dhal

2/3 cup green moong dhal
1 onion, chopped
1 tsp. minced ginger
4 large garlic cloves minced fine
2 large tomatoes, sliced
1 tsp. cumin powder
1 tsp. coriander powder
1 tsp. Garam Masala powder (optional)
1 tsp. turmeric powder
2 tsp. salt or to taste

Directions:
Pre-cook the lentils using three cups of water. Heat oil in a saucepan and fry the cumin seeds for a minute. Add the chopped onions, minced ginger, minced garlic, cumin, coriander and Garam Masala powders, as well as sliced tomatoes and cook, stirring constantly, for ten minutes on medium low heat.

Stir in lentils with another three cups of water and turmeric powder, heat till the mixture starts boiling, season with salt and remove from heat.

Green Beans (Gujerati)

1 lb. fresh green beans
4 tablespoons vegetable oil
1 tablespoon black mustard seed
4 cloves garlic, peeled and finely chopped
1 hot red dried chilli, crushed
1 teaspoon salt
1/2 teaspoon granulated sugar
Black pepper to taste

Directions:
Trim the beans and cut into 1.inch lengths. Blanch by dropping them into a pot of boiling water and boiling rapidly for 3 to 4 minutes. Drain in a colander, rinse under cold running water and set aside. Heat the oil in a large frying pan over medium heat. When hot, add mustard seeds. As soon as they begin to pop, add garlic and stir until lightly brown.

Add crushed red chilli and stir for a few seconds. Add green beans, salt and sugar. Stir to mix. Turn heat to medium/low. Stir and cook the beans for 7 to 8 minutes until they have absorbed the spiced flavors. Add black pepper, mix and serve.

Okra Curry - (Masala Bhindi)

1 lb. okra, sliced lengthwise or chopped into small pieces.
2 onions, pureed
2 tsp. ginger paste
2 tsp. garlic paste
1 tsp. turmeric
1 tsp. chilli powder
1 tsp. cumin powder
1 tsp. coriander powder
1 potato, cubed
1 tsp. salt or to taste
1 large tomato, pureed
2 tbsp. oil

Directions:
Heat oil in a non-stick frying pan (or skillet) and fry the onions, ginger and garlic, together with cumin and coriander powders and tomato for five minutes on medium low heat. Add potato, okra, turmeric and chilli
powders and salt and cook on medium low heat for half an hour.

Peas Pulao - Vegetarian

1 1/4 cup uncooked rice
1 tsp. turmeric powder
1 tsp. chilli powder
1 tsp. each cumin and mustard seeds
1 tsp. salt or to taste
Cilantro/coriander leaves
1 tbsp. oil
For the peas:
1 lb. shelled green peas
1 tsp. ginger paste
1 tsp. garlic paste
1 tsp. turmeric powder
1 tsp. chilli powder
1 tsp. cumin seeds
1 tsp. salt or to taste
Cilantro/coriander leaves
1 tbsp. oil

Directions:
Heat oil in a heavy bottomed saucepan and fry the cumin and mustard seeds for one minute. Add rice, turmeric and chilli powders and salt together with two and a half cups of lukewarm water, cover with the lid
and cook on medium low heat for half an hour.

While the rice is cooking, heat oil in a non-stick frying pan (or skillet) and fry the cumin seeds, together with ginger and garlic, for five minutes. Add green peas, turmeric and chilli powders and salt together with half
a cup of lukewarm water and cook on medium low heat for fifteen minutes. Garnish with cilantro/coriander leaves. When the rice is done, mix the peas and garnish with cilantro/coriander leaves.

Poha

2 cups flattened rice (poha) available at any Indian grocery store.
2 cups water
1 potato, chopped small
2 tablespoons ghee
1 onion, chopped fine
1/4 cup groundnuts (raw peanuts)
1/2 teaspoon turmeric (just enough to colour the rice)
1/2 teaspoon mustard seeds
Lemon juice, to taste
Salt and pepper

Directions:
Soak the flattened rice (poha) in water and set aside.
In a large round bottomed frying pan, heat the ghee till very hot. Add mustard seeds, onion, potato and groundnuts. When the mustard seeds are tender, cover with water and cook till potato and groundnuts are tender.

Drain off any excess water from the soaked rice. Add the turmeric to the rice until it's a nice golden yellow. Add the rice to the frying pan and mix with the potato onion mixture until hot. Add salt, pepper and lemon juice to your taste.

DESERTS AND PUDDINGS

India has a large repertoire of sweets. Each region has its own specialties. Basically, Indian sweets are different forms of rice puddings, milk puddings, vegetables & fruits dipped in sweet syrup. Besides, there are varieties of fudge like sweets called Barfis. Indian sweets are decorated or garnished with raisins, almonds, pistachio and the like.

Some other popular Indian sweets are:- Kheer, Halwa (pudding), Rasgulla (spongy cheese balls, dipped in sugar syrup), Gulab Jamun, Rasmalai, Sandesh and ladoos. 'Kulfi' is the Indian version of Ice-cream.

Most Indian sweets are made by boiling down milk to remove the moisture. It is called khoa. Adding butter, sugar and many other flavours, these are turned into barfi, malai, kheer, rasgulla and sandesh.

SANDESH

Ingredients
Fresh chenna of cows milk 350 gm
Sugar 50-75 gm
Small cardamom powder ¼ tsp
Rose water Few drops
Pista (for garnishing)

METHOD

- Rub the chenna with palm until smooth.
- Add sugar.
- Cook in a kadhai on a slow fire, until it leaves the side of pan.
- Remove from fire.
- Add flavouring.
- Make small peadas and garnish with pista.

KESARI KHEER

Ingredients
Milk   1.5 litres
Kesar   2 gm

Rice	150 gm
Rose Water	Few drops
Ghee	15 gm
Almonds	20 gm
Sugar	125 gm
Kaju	20 gm
Green cardamom	5 gm
Kishmish	15 gm

METHOD

- Wash and soak rice for four hours.
- Blanch almonds and remove the skin.
- Dissolve saffron in milk boil milk in a handy.
- Heat fat and fry the rice.
- Add milk and stir continuously.
- Reduce heat and slimmer on slow fire till the rice is looked.
- Add sugar and cook till fairly thick.
- Add remaining ingredients and serve hot.

GULAB JAMUN

INGREDIENTS

Mawa	75 gms
Sodium bicarbonate	A pinch
Sugar	75 gms
Fat	For frying
Cardamom	2 nos.
Rose Water	Few drops
Arrarot	10 gms
Water	35 ml

METHOD

- Prepare a sugar syrup of one string consistently with water.
- Sugar and rose water. Pass the Mawa through a strainer.
- Add crushed cardamom sieved arrarot and little cold water in which soda bi-carbonate has been dissolved.
- Make a soft clough without reading
- Divide into equal portion and shape into small balls. Fry into a deep fat till brown.

- Frying should be done on slow fire and it should be stirred constantly.
- Remove, cool for a short while and put in cold syrup.

MOONG DAL KA HALWA

INGREDIENTS

Ingredients	Qty
Split green gram	150 gm
Milk	150 gm
Sugar	200 gm
Fat	100 gm

For Decorating : Almond, colour, cardamom, cashew nuts.

METHOD

- Soak the gram for 4-5 hours.
- Grind into a very fine paste.
- Melt fat in kadhai and add grounded gram.
- Fry to a slight brown colour over a very slow fire.
- Boil milk separately with sugar.
- When gram starts browning, add milk on it and keep stirring till all the milk gets dried up and fat starts boozing out from the halwa.
- Remove and serve hot.
- Garnish with dry fruits.

SHAHI TUKDA

INGREDIENTS

Ingredients	Qty
Bread slices	4 no.
Sugar	400 ml
Milk	300 ml
Cardamom	30 no.

Saffron	A pinch
Cashew nut	15 gm
Pistachio	15 gm
Oil(deep fry)	15 gm

METHOD

- Heat fat and fry slices of bread, remove.
- Boil the milk, simmer and reduce to half.
- Add sugar and boil for another 10 min's.
- Heat saffron and soak in a little milk.
- Pour on a fried bread.
- Arrange in a tray without over lapping
- Pour the milk over the bread
- Garnish with cashew nut, cardamom etc.
- Serve hot

MOHAN THAL

INGREDIENTS

Besan	115gms
Pistachio	30gms
Milk	60ml
Cardamom	17nos
Fat	170gms
Sugar	340gms

METHOD

- Mix Gram flour with milk and 55gms fat.
- Make a thick sugar syrup.
- Blanch and slice almonds and pistachio.
- Add powdered cardamom.
- Heat the remaining fat. Add besan and than fry.
- Add sugar syrup. Mix well. Remove and pour into a guessed tray and allow to set.
- Sprinkle cardamom powder.
- Garnish with nuts and cut into piece.

MAWA KACHORI

INGREDIENTS

Ingredients	Qty	Ingredients	Qty	Ingredients	Qty
		For filling		For Syrup	
Maida	½ kg	Mawa	½ kg	Sugar	½ kg
Fat	125 gm	Sugar	50 gm	Water	400 ml
Salt	A pinch	Chirongi	25 gm	lemon	2-3
Baking powder	¼ tsp	Cardamom	5 gm	Rose water	Few
Water	Making dough	Cashew nut			50 gm

METHOD

- Sieve flour, salt and baking powder. Rub the melted fat and knead it to a medium soft dough using water.
- Keep it aside, fry mawa till it starts changing the colour.
- Remove from fire and let it cool and add powdered sugar, Cardamom powder, and nuts.
- Mix well, divide the dough into to equal sized balls. Roll out each ball to 3 inch diameter
- Place the filling on the 20 portion and cover each with the remaining 20.
- Seal the edges, deep fry to just a pink colour on a slow fire.
- Prepare the sugar syrup. Dip the fired kachori serve either hot or cold.

PHIRNEE

INGREDIENTS

Ingredients	Qty
Rice flour	30gm
Sugar	60gtm
Milk	300ml
Almonds	15gm
Pistachio nuts	10gm
Cardamom	A pinch

METHOD

- Mix Rice flour with a little cold milk
- Boil remaining milk, add to rice flour mixture.
- Cook on a slow fire, till it becomes fairly thick
- Draw the pan to the side of the fire and sprinkle sugar.
- When sugar is dissolved powder.
- Pour into flat dishes. Recorded with shredded Nuts.
- Cool and serve.

GAJAR KA HALWA

INGREDIENTS

Carrot	250gm
Milk	100gm
Mawa	250gm
Clarified butter	55gm
Sugar	115gm
Dry fruits	20gm
Cardamom	5gm

METHOD

- Wash carrot, peel and grate
- Add carrot to the milk and cook
- When milk dries, add fat and fry.
- Add half Mawa and cook
- Add sugar, add dry fruits and crushed cardamom
- Sprinkle over with left over Mawa

SUJI HALWA

Ingredients	Qty
Semolina	100 gm
Sugar	100 gm
Fat	40 gm
Cardamom	4-5 no.
Water	200-300 ml.

METHOD

- Melt fat and roast semolina. Till it is light brown.
- Add hot water and mix well.
- Keep the pan cover for 2 min.
- Add sugar and mix well
- Add cardamom powder.
- Cook for 5 min. till all the sugar melts.
- Remove from fire and serve.

Shrikhand

This is a simple Indian dessert from Western India, made with strained yogurt and flavoured with cardamom, and saffron and garnished with almonds and pista. It is important to use freshly ground cardamom seeds.

Ingredients: Servings 4 to 6
1 quart whole milk yogurt
1/3 cup powdered sugar
1/3 tsp. cardamom powder
few strands saffron
1/2 tbsp. pista & almond crushed

Method:
Tie yogurt in a clean muslin cloth overnight. (6-7 hours).
Put the yogurt into a bowl, add sugar and cardamom and mix.
Rub saffron into 1 tbsp. hot milk, in a small bowl, until the colour spreads and dissolved and add to the yogurt

Empty into a serving bowl, and garnish with nut crush.
Chill for 1-2 hours before serving.

Kheer

For 1 or 2 per person.

Ingredients
1/2 cup basmati rice
2 cups water
2 quarts milk
5 green cardamom pods ground
1 1/4 cups sugar
1/4 cup slivered blanched almonds
1/2 tsp. ground cardamom
1/4 tsp. ground nutmeg
1 Tbs. rose water

Method:
1 Wash the rice and boil in the water over medium heat for 5 to 6 minutes, until the rice is one quarter done. Drain in a colander.
2. In a saucepan, bring the milk and cardamom pods to a boil over medium heat. Add the rice and cook for 30 to 40 minutes, until the rice is soft and the milk is very thick. Stir occasionally at first and then constantly when the milk begins to thicken, to prevent the ingredients from sticking to the bottom of the pan.
3. Add the sugar, almonds, ground cardamom, and nutmeg and cook for another 5 minutes, stirring constantly.
4. Remove from the heat and set aside. Sprinkle with the rose water.
5. Serve warm or chilled in dessert bowls.

Carrot Halwa

Ingredients:
1 lb. Carrots peeled and thinly grated and sautéed in ghee
Half and Half 1 pint
Sugar to taste sugar
4 Cardamom pods ground
Raisins handful
Cashew nuts handful
Ghee

Method:
1. Add a little ghee to a frying pan and heat to coat the pan. Roast cashew nuts until golden brown and add the raisins to the pan for a few seconds. Remove the cashews and raisins and keep aside.
2. Add the carrots to the pan and sauté the carrots. Add Half and Half, and heat for about an hour. Add cardamom and starting with medium heat, stirring, and lowering the heat after the mixture starts boiling. Heat until almost dry.
3. Add sugar, mix, and continue to cook until the carrot halwa is semi dry.
4. Remove from stove and add cashews and raisins.

Sheera

Ingredients:
1 cup semolina (or cream of wheat)
1/4 cup sugar or more to taste
1/2 cup ghee (clarified butter)
3 cups water
1/2 tsp. cardamom powder, chopped nuts (like cashew nuts and almonds) and raisins

Method:
Heat ghee (clarified butter) in a pan on medium level till it is hot. Add semolina. Stir well and fry on low heat for 7 minutes or till the semolina is lightly roasted. Keep aside
Mix the sugar, cardamom and water in a vessel. Bring to boil and keep on medium / low heat uncovered for 2 minute(s) stirring periodically.
Now add the water mixture. Stir well. Bring to boil and turn heat on low immediately. Keep on low heat, stirring periodically (after every minute) till the mixture is dry.
Sprinkle chopped nuts and raisins. Serve with a dollop of ice-cream.

Kahara Prasad

a variation of the above recipe - This prasad or temple offering is given in Sikh temples during the full moon day around October-November when Guru Nanak was born, and during Guru Parab, the birthday of Guru Gobind Singh. It is a day when they rededicate themselves to unity, brotherhood and equality among all human beings. After all this religion was created to bring Hindus and Muslims together.

Ingredients:
5 cups rava or coarsely ground wheat flour or mixture of both
5 cups ghee
5 cups sugar

Method:
Heat ghee and add the rava or the flour. Fry, stirring constantly, till each grain is brown. Add sugar little by little and continue cooking till ghee separates and the sugar is blended. No flavouring must be added. Serve hot

---

Seviyan

Ingredients
6 nos. Dry dates
1 tablespoon Raisins
1 tablespoon Cashew nuts
1 tablespoon Sunflower seeds
1 tablespoon Blanched almonds
1 tablespoon Blanched pistachio
2 1/2 tablespoons Ghee
1/4 cup Vermicelli
4 cups Milk
2 teaspoons Cardamom powder
3 1/2 tablespoons Sugar

Method:
Soak the dates overnight. De-seed and chop into 4 pieces.
Heat ghee and sauté the raisins, cashew nuts, chironji seeds, almonds and pistachios for 2-3 minutes. Drain and mix with the chopped dry dates. Set aside.
In the same ghee, fry the vermicelli on a low flame for about 2 minutes, stirring continuously. Remove from heat and keep aside.
Boil the milk in a deep bottomed pan and add the vermicelli and sugar. Stir until the sugar dissolves. Cook uncovered on a low flame for about 10 minutes, stirring often. Add the fried dry fruits and cardamom powder, cover and cook for 3 minutes.
Serve hot or cold in individual bowls.

Kalakand

Ingredients:

2 cups full fat milk
1 cup cottage cheese
1/2 cup sugar

Directions:
Boil milk in a heavy bottomed saucepan until it reduces to half. Add cottage cheese and sugar and mix well till it attains a semi solid consistency. Preheat the oven. Transfer the mixture to a square shaped oven proof dish and bake at 425F for 10 minutes. Let stand in the oven for half and hour. Cut into squares and serve.

Rice Pudding (Payesh)

Ingredients

1/2 gallon full fat milk
2 cups cooked rice
1 cup raisins
1/2 cup sugar

Directions
Boil milk in a heavy bottomed saucepan until it reduces to half. The key to this dessert is vigilant, constant stirring to ensure that the contents do not stick to the bottom of the vessel. Add cooked rice, raisins and sugar and mix well till it attains a thick sticky consistency

DRINKS

In North India, temperatures in summer can reach 110° and stay there for some time. India has devised many chillers to stay cool like lassi, Thandai, shiquanji, cold coffee and other nut shakes with cardamom the Indian answer to vanilla. So next time you want to reach out for a cola try one of India's exotic coolers.
If you are entertaining we suggest our canned Mango or Lychee syrup for making a Lychee or Mango drinks or lassi. They are tasty and convenient to make. Hospitality in India is expressed with offering tea or coffee with sweets and savoury snacks. Families in India are also partial to many hot milk drinks flavoured with ginger, cardamom, nutmeg, fennel, saffron and fortified with nuts and seeds to create a powerful protein drink.

Sweet Lassi

Ingredients:

1 Serving
Plain yogurt- 1 cup
Sugar- 2 tablespoons
Ice Cubes- 4

Method:
Blend all the ingredients in an electric blender. Serve cold.

Mango Lassi

Mango lassi is a favourite at Indian restaurants. Now you can make some in your own kitchen.

Ingredients: 2 Serving
1 cup plain yogurt
1cup peeled and chopped ripe mango
or 1/2 cup mango pulp
sugar or to taste (less if pulp is used)
1/4th tsp. cardamom powder (optional)
Few ice-cubes

Method:
Combine all ingredients and blend until smooth in a blender.

Strain through a sieve, pushing as much liquid as possible. If the pulp has been used there is no need to strain.
Pour in glasses and serve.

Cold Coffee

Indian cold coffee is sweet and refreshing. Use instant coffee with chicory or Camp coffee and the hot coffee to the milk and ice to the coffee, allowing it to cascade through.

Ingredients:
5 cups cold milk preferably whole
1/2 cup boiling water
6 tsp. instant coffee powder
3 tbsp. sugar crushed ice

Method
Dissolve instant coffee powder and sugar in boiling water and allow to cool.
Blend the coffee mixture and milk in a blender for few seconds.
Add cream and crushed ice. Blend for another few seconds till it becomes frothy.
Serve chilled.

Nut Milk or Thandai

When North India is bristling under its hot summers and one is not inclined to cook or eat much families enjoy Thandai. It is both a healthful and refreshing drink. It is also popular for festive occasions and served while entertaining guests. It is a popular drink at elaborate Indian weddings.

Ingredients:
2 glasses of whole milk
1 cup water
1 tablespoon blanched almonds
1 tablespoon Pistachios
1 tablespoon Poppy Seeds
6 cashew nuts
Powdered cardamom, Cinnamon, Nutmeg- a pinch each
Honey as per taste

Method
Bring the water to boil in a small sauce pan. Add the spices. Remove from heat and set aside to cool for 10 minutes.
Make a fine paste of all the nuts and poppy seeds along with the heated spices. Pour into a strainer lined with a damp cloth and set over a clean bowl. Squeeze all the milk out of the nuts by tightening the cloth by wringing it. You may use the nut pulp for thickening Indian curries or in baking.
Mix this paste with the other spices into the milk and stir well. Mix the honey and chill. Serve in glasses with crushed ice.

Mango Milk Shake

Ingredients:
2 cup mango pulp from a can or flesh of 3 ripe mangoes
6 cups milk
3 Tbsp. sugar for canned mango pulp. More sugar if fresh mangoes used.
10 crushed ice cubes
Method:
Blend all the ingredients in a blender. Serve cold.
The "mango nectar" that is widely available in grocery stores does not have nearly enough mangoes per unit volume to make this drink.

Aloo Bonda

Ingredients: 4 Serving
2 cups water
3 whole cloves
1 stick cinnamon
3 to 4 cardamom pods (cracked open)
1/4 cup loose black tea (or 4 tea bags)
2 cups milk
4 tablespoons of sugar (or a little less)

Method:
Bring water, cloves, cinnamon and cardamom to a boil; Add tea and milk and bring to a boil. When hot, strain and add sugar. Serve hot.

Cardamom Milk- Elaichi Doodh

This drink is popular in the plains of North India and in Bengal.   Can also double up as a light meal before bed. Makes a healthy warming hot milk or a sweet after dinner drink or a filling milk drink before bed (especially when one has had an early supper). A warm nut milkshake

Ingredients:
3 tbsp. white poppy seeds dry roasted in a pan
15 blanched almonds
1 cup water
3 cups whole milk
1 tablespoon Poppy Seeds
1/2 tsp. cardamom seeds
sugar to taste
Method

1. Dry roast poppy seeds in a heavy frying pan over low heat. stirring the pan often so as not to burn it, for about 5 minutes. Combine the poppy seeds, almonds and water in a blender or food processor fitted with the metal blade and process for 2-3 minutes or until the nuts are reduced to a fine puree. Add 2 cups milk and further blend on low speed for about 15 seconds.
2. Pour the mixture through a strainer over a pan. Press out as much liquid as possible, then add the remaining milk and the cardamom seeds. Stirring constantly, bring to a boil over moderately high heat. Reduce the heat to low and simmer for 2 minutes. Add the sweetener.
3. Indians will pour the milk back and forth from one pan to another to make the milk frothy much like a low tech cappuccino machine. The frothy milk is then served.

Almond Honey Milk - Madhur Badam Doodh

In the cold winter months of North India many families wake up to an almond au lait. The milk is warming, protein rich and all natural and enjoyed by the whole family - grandparents, parents and children

Ingredients:
1/2 cup blanched almonds
2 cups milk
1/4 teaspoon of cardamom powder or 1/2 tsp. vanilla.
honey or sugar to taste
Method:

1. Add almonds and water in a blender or food processor fitted with the metal blade and process for 2-3 minutes or until the nuts are reduced to a fine puree. Add 2 cups of milk and further blend on low speed for about 15 seconds. Heat the milk blend to a boil.
2. Pour the mixture through a strainer over a pan. Press out as much liquid as possible, then add the cardamom seeds. Stirring constantly, bring to a near boil over moderately high heat. Reduce the heat to low and simmer for 2 minutes. Add the sweetener.
3. Indians will pour the milk back and forth from one pan to another to make the milk frothy much like a low tech cappuccino machine. The frothy milk is then served. Nice with a slice of banana as well.

Yogurt Mint Drink (Lassi)

Mix together:
1 quart milk
1 quart plain yogurt
to cup sugar, or a combination of sugar and honey
4 teaspoons vanilla

Yogurt Mint Drink Recipe Directions:
Immerse into lassi: 6 to 8 fresh mint stalks (bruise leaves and tie ends of stalks together) or 2 to 3 tablespoons dried mint in a tea ball or cheesecloth. Let stand in refrigerator at least 5 hours to allow the mint to flavour the lassi. Remove mint before serving.
Makes 2 quarts.